PLUGGED IN: HIGH VOLTAGE

PRAYER

Accessing The Power of God Through Prayer

EDWIN CROZIER

SECOND EDITION: STUDY MATERIAL INCLUDED

ISBN 0-9777829-5-6

All scripture quotations, unless otherwise indicated, are taken from the New King James Version ®. Copyright © 1982 by Thomas Nelson, Inc. Used by permission. All rights reserved.

Scriptures marked (NASB) are taken from the New American Standard Bible®, Copyright © 1960, 1962, 1963, 1968, 1971, 1972, 1973, 1975, 1977, 1995 by the Lockman Foundation. Used by permission.

To order additional copies:
Write to Streamside Supplies; 95 Oak Valley Dr. Spring Hill, TN, 37174;
Or call (877) 644-3225 and request Streamside Supplies.
www.streamsidesupplies.com

Cover design by Phillip Shumake

Printed in the United States of America

Other Works by Edwin Crozier

Books

Built by the Lord: A Study of the Family

The Gospel of the Kingdom: Studies in the Sermon on the Mount

Walks with God

Give Attention to Reading

Available for order wherever books are sold.
Or direct from the publisher at
www.streamsidesupplies.com

DVD

Your First 10 Days as a Christian

Available directly from the publisher at
www.streamsidesupplies.com

Acknowledgments

I am grateful to the Franklin Church of Christ for allowing me to present this material to them in raw form. Their support and encouragement pushed this material from private study to congregational teaching to public resource.

I want to offer special thanks to Steve and Carla Duffy, whose persistence bolstered me to complete this book. I will forever be indebted to you.

I want to thank my wife, Marita, who has put up with me as I repeatedly and excitedly told her where this material was going. As God said, "Two are better than one." Thank you.

I want to thank Phillip Shumake, whose hard work has made this new edition look like the book I always envisioned.

Finally, I must thank God for granting me this opportunity to study, learn and help others grow.

O Lord, May You be blessed and glorified in my life and with this book.

Plugged In: High Voltage Prayer

Table of Contents

Introduction

As the third millennium broke upon our world, an often overlooked Old Testament hero was thrust into the limelight. Despite the number of times we had read or glanced over the first chapters of **I Chronicles**, most of us skimmed past Jabez. Bruce Wilkinson's little book, *__The Prayer of Jabez__*, made the two verse champion and his tiny prayer a force with which to be reckoned.

I have little desire to enter into the debate surrounding that volume. There were some things I liked about Wilkinson's book. There were some things I did not like. However, I will be eternally grateful for the introduction to Jabez.

"Now Jabez was more honorable than his brothers, and his mother called his name Jabez, saying, 'Because I bore him in pain.' And Jabez called on the God of Israel saying, 'Oh, that You would bless me indeed, and enlarge my territory, that Your hand would be with me, and that You would keep me from evil, that I may not cause pain!' So God granted him what he requested" (**I Chronicles 4:9-10**).

As God ran through the droning roll call of humanity, He stopped and said, "Hey everybody, check out this guy. This is my servant."

When God picked out the prime example of the servant He honors, He did not pinpoint his property, predecessors or prowess. Instead, God honored Jabez' prayer.

That stunned me. Do not miss the forest for the trees. The most important part of these two verses is not what Jabez prayed, but that he prayed. The most important statement in **I Chronicles 4:9-10** is "And Jabez called on the God of Israel."

The Chronicler was going to tell the stories of many Israelites. Every single one of them could be judged based on how they compared to Jabez and his prayer. Did they, like Jabez, pray to the living God, or did they, like Rehoboam in **II Chronicles 11:15**, pray to dead idols? Did they, like Jabez, pray to the God of Israel, or did they, like Amaziah in **II Chronicles 25:14**, pray to foreign gods? If they prayed like Jabez, they were blessed like Jabez. If not, they were cursed.

But Jabez is dead and gone. His territory is being fought over in the terror stricken Middle East. Why should I care about these two verses? Because God still looks for praying servants.

When I came face to face with Jabez, I was forced to ask myself a question. If God were to call the universe's attention to me, could He even remotely say anything about my prayer life? When I asked this, the echoing answer in my heart was a deadening "No."

Do not misunderstand. Since becoming a Christian in my early teens, I had prayed nearly every day. I had always blessed every meal, even when in front of unbelievers. I had said "night-night" prayers with all of my children since the time they were old enough for me to hold them.

2

But I suddenly realized my prayers were no more than ritual. I prayed because I knew I should, not because I truly believed they accomplished anything. Therefore, I did not pray very much.

I often told people I would pray for them, but that statement had about as much meaning as when I asked, "How are you doing today?" It was the polite Christian thing to say, but I really did not mean it. Certainly, I had times when prayer was more meaningful. But as with most New Year's resolutions, the commitment would wear off in a few weeks.

There was Jabez staring me in the face. Something had to be done. I must learn to pray.

I have come a long way since 2000. I still do not think I am at Jabez' prayer level. I know I am not at Jesus' prayer level. However I have grown, and I am still growing.

The volume you hold in your hands right now is the result of my study and growth. It is not the end of my study on prayer. It is the beginning.

Over the past years, I have learned prayer is not one of the privileges we have been given. It is not one of the works we perform. It is THE privilege. It is THE work. It is the beginning of every endeavor in God's work, the connection that carries us through and the conclusion of every success we have through God's grace.

If you are already a fervent prayer, I invite you to join me in this study simply to prompt greater understanding and to affirm and support you in your devotion. If, however, you are like I have been, I invite you to join me as we learn to plug in to the power of the universe—God. If you take the teaching from God's word found in this book to heart, I believe you will be well on your way to fervent, effective, High Voltage Prayer.

3

As we study prayer together, I am not interested in rehashing old prayer traditions. Therefore, this book will not be about what we have always done in prayer.

At the same time, I am not interested in destroying traditions. This study is not designed to pass on some new-fangled prayer gimmicks I think I have discovered.

Additionally, I have learned that our prayer experiences are pretty pointless when it comes to a true study on prayer. This book is not about the "successful" prayers I have prayed. It is not filled with testimonials of people who must have prayed right because, "Look at what God did for them." It is not about how real prayer makes us feel. Rather, we will look at the word of God and see what it says about prayer.

I am convinced we will be praying properly, not when we pray like we always have, not when we pray differently than we always have, not when we are getting what we want, not when we feel like we are praying, but when we are praying the way God teaches in His word.

When my friend, Ralph Walker, preaches on prayer, he points out that Jesus was the greatest teacher and preacher ever. Yet, the disciples never pulled Him aside and said, "Lord, teach us to teach." Or, "Lord, teach us to preach." They did, however, pull Jesus aside and say, "Lord, teach us to pray" (**Luke 11:1**).

Prayer was important to Jesus. Prayer was important to His apostles. Prayer must be important to us.

Please, read this book with an open Bible. This book is not inspired. Nor is it God's prayer manual. However, each chapter is filled with God's inspired scripture. You will get the most out of this study, not by simply reading my words, but by reading God's word upon which they are based.

I am well aware that this book does not answer all the possible questions regarding prayer. What book could accomplish

4

that? Nor will it make us perfect prayers. How could it do that? However, I firmly believe our study together will glorify God as we plug in to Him, growing in High Voltage Prayer.

May God bless us as we grow. More importantly, may God be blessed as we grow.

Plugged In: High Voltage Prayer

WEEK ONE

"Therefore take up the whole armor of God that you may be able to withstand in the evil day, and having done all, to stand. Stand therefore…praying always with all prayer and supplication in the Spirit, being watchful to this end with all perseverance and supplication for all the saints."

Ephesians 6:13-14, 18

Chapter 1

So, You Want To Be A Prayer Warrior?

Real Warriors

The Philistines had attacked and Israel retreated. No doubt the battlefield was littered with the remains of dead Israelites and the Philistines glorying over their prey.

But three men stood in the gap. They were David's three mighty men; and they had had enough.

Adino the Eznite killed eight hundred men at one time.

Eleazar the Ahohite fought the Philistines until his hand was so wearied and cramped he could not relax it enough to release his sword. But the Israelites who returned to the battle-field had no one left to fight.

Shammah the Hararite single-handedly defended a field against a troop of Philistines.

These men were not fighting alone. They were plugged in to the real power. Therefore, the Bible says "the Lord brought about a great victory" through these warriors (**II Samuel 23:8-12**).

Move over Conan. Get out of the way Rambo. We have found some real warriors. Wouldn't you like to be like these guys?

You can be. No, this is not about becoming the next Terminator. We are talking about spiritual warriors. Do not be deceived. The world may look peaceful to you. It may seem that war is something we only hear about on the news, happening in distant countries. Regrettably, war is taking place all around us.

Ephesians 6:12 says, "We do not wrestle against flesh and blood, but against principalities, against powers, against the rulers of the darkness of this age, against spiritual hosts of wickedness in the heavenly places."

The devil and his hellish forces are real and we are engaged in a battle with them. We must make sure we do not get so caught up in looking at the material prosperity around us that we forget we are walking through a battlefield. Regrettably, the great majority of the world, even the religious world, is in retreat.

God needs some mighty men and women to stand in the gap. He needs Christians to stand up, perhaps I should say kneel down, and pray like warriors.

Praying Warriors

I do not know who first coined the phrase "Prayer Warriors," but I love it. It lets us know exactly what we are doing when we pray. We are fighting a fight. We are standing on the battlefield with our hands cramped around our sword, allowing God to bring about victories through us.

Prayer is not a useless or last resort activity. I am saddened to think about the times I have said with resignation, "Well, I guess all we can do is pray." That makes about as much sense as Eleazar looking to Shammah and Adino and saying, "Well, I guess all we can do is stomp some Philistines."

However, as much as I like the phrase, I am not sure it accurately portrays what we Christians are. Read **Ephesians 6:13-18**.

Therefore take up the whole armor of God, that you may be able to withstand in the evil day, and having done all, to stand. Stand therefore, having girded your waist with truth, having put on the breastplate of righteousness, and having shod your feet with the preparation of the gospel of peace; above all, taking the shield of faith with which you will be able to quench all the fiery darts of the wicked one. And take the helmet of salvation, and the sword of the Spirit, which is the word of God; praying always with all prayer and supplication in the Spirit, being watchful to this end with all perseverance and supplication for all the saints.

We are not really prayer warriors. Rather, we are God's warriors whose armor is completed by prayer. A better phrase might be "Praying Warriors." Without prayer, our armor is incomplete, filled with holes through which the enemy can nail us with his fiery darts.

We can never be strong warriors without prayer, but we must realize our fight is not finished when we pray. Rather, our armor is secured by prayer.

11

I admit, all this talk about wars, warriors and fiery darts is a little frightening. I would like to be a Praying Warrior, but right now I have a hard time even being a Praying Private.

If you feel like this—it's OK. We do not come out of the watery grave fully grown. Prayer is a growth process. A passage to which I look for comfort is **II Peter 1:5-8**.

But also for this very reason, giving all diligence, add to your faith virtue, to virtue knowledge, to knowledge self-control, to self-control perseverance, to perseverance godliness, to godliness brotherly kindness, and to brotherly kindness love. For if these things are yours and abound, you will be neither barren nor unfruitful in the knowledge of our Lord Jesus Christ.

God's standards for us are high. We cannot sit on the side of the battlefield. However, God will not give us the dishonorable discharge just because we are not perfect fighting machines. He simply wants us to be better today than we were yesterday. He wants us to be better tomorrow than we are today.

We can do that, can't we? Remember **Philippians 4:13**? "I can do all things through Christ who strengthens me."

Basic Training

Here is the crux of the matter. Becoming a warrior takes training and development. If we joined the U. S. Army, we would not go straight to the battlefield. We would first go through Basic Training to be trained physically and to be taught our jobs.

All of this would be necessary to make us warriors. It works very much the same way in the Lord's army. We will not become warriors overnight. We need training.

This book will not answer all your questions about prayer. Nor will it provide all the training you will ever need to be a Praying Warrior. However, it will be Basic Training, helping you develop the disciplines and understanding you need to begin your workout and progress.

In time, if you continue to rely on God, trust His word and grow in His will, you will be able to say that you are a Praying Warrior.

However, it all begins right now. Are you committed to prayer? Are you committed to growth in prayer? In the Army's basic training, someone else would wake you up and run you through your drills. It will not work that way here. You must develop your own commitment. However, you can get help. **Ecclesiastes 4:9** says, "Two are better than one." I encourage you to find a friend with whom to read this book. Let each other know what your commitments to prayer are and then hold one another accountable. However you approach this study, determine right now when you will pray today.

Prayer Challenge

Making your commitment:

For this study to do you any good, you must be committed. No doubt, you can read through the entire book in just a few sittings and learn a great deal about prayer. But this book is not just about learning how to pray; it is about praying. Therefore, you need to make a daily commitment. Consider the commitments you need to make for this to be a successful study. Obviously all plans need to be flexible, but you at least need a target plan.

When will you read this book each day?

When will you pray each day?

With whom will you share this goal so they can help hold you accountable?

When will you talk with them and how can they hold you accountable?

Ephesians 6:13-18 describes the armor of God. What does that armor mean to you and how do you think prayer fits in with the rest of the armor?

Plug In:

Father in heaven,

Thank You for forgiving me through Your Son's blood. Thank You for accepting me where I am and helping me grow to be what You want me to be.

Father, I desire to be a Praying Warrior in Your army. Please, strengthen me that I may glorify You at all times. Please, help me be Your instrument through which You can accomplish great victories.

I love You, Father.

In Your Son's name I pray,

Amen

Chapter 2

Lord, Teach Us To Pray

Teach Us To Pray

Luke 11:1-13.

1 Now it came to pass, as He was praying in a certain place, when He ceased, that one of His disciples said to Him, "Lord, teach us to pray, as John also taught his disciples."

2 So He said to them, "When you pray, say: Our Father in heaven, Hallowed be Your name. Your kingdom come. Your will be done On earth as it is in heaven.

3 Give us day by day our daily bread.

4 And forgive us our sins, For we also forgive everyone who is indebted to us. And do not lead us into temptation, But deliver us from the evil one."

5 And He said to them, "Which of you shall have a friend, and go to him at midnight and say to him, 'Friend, lend me three loaves;

6 'for a friend of mine has come to me on his journey, and I have nothing to set before him';

7 "and he will answer from within and say, 'Do not trouble me; the door is now shut, and my children are with me in bed; I cannot rise and give to you'?

8 "I say to you, though he will not rise and give to him because he is his friend, yet because of his persistence he will rise and give him as many as he needs.

9 "So I say to you, ask, and it will be given to you; seek, and you will find; knock, and it will be opened to you.

10 "For everyone who asks receives, and he who seeks finds, and to him who knocks it will be opened.

11 "If a son asks for bread from any father among you, will he give him a stone? Or if he asks for a fish, will he give him a serpent instead of a fish?

12 "Or if he asks for an egg, will he offer him a scorpion?

13 "If you then, being evil, know how to give good gifts to your children, how much more will your heavenly Father give the Holy Spirit to those who ask Him!"

Have you ever felt as the disciples did? How many times had they heard the Master pray? How many times did they know He had spent all night praying? How often had they thought, "I wish I could pray like that"?

One day, they worked up the nerve to ask, "Lord, teach us to pray."

What a great step of spiritual growth to know we must learn to pray. One of my best friends confided to me about the day he knew he was spiritually bankrupt. At a secular meeting, he was asked to lead prayer and realized he did not know how.

In time, he became a Christian and did learn. He is now a bishop in the Lord's church and teaches others to pray. His spiritual growth began with the recognition that he needed to learn to pray. I am convinced that is when spiritual growth really begins for all of us.

I hope you read the entire Bible passage provided above. However, we are going to focus on lessons we can gather for our prayer lives from the apostles' simple request, "Lord, teach us to pray."

Prayer Is Not Natural

I remember the day my wife and I became disgusted with a parenting magazine to which we had subscribed. Its constant refrain was for a mother to follow her instincts. But its advice allowed the child to rule the roost. I do not know everything about parenting, but I am pretty sure the parents are supposed to be in control. We finally learned in parenting, if we did what came naturally, we were probably doing it wrong.

To a certain degree, the same is true with prayer. (Do not get upset thinking we cannot pray until we have finished a college level course in proper prayer. We will balance this out by the end of this chapter.)

Carefully note Jesus' response. He did not reply, "Just say whatever comes naturally." Nor did He say, "Just talk to God like you do your best friend." These clichés may be a starting place. But they do not contain everything we need to know about prayer.

In fact, **Ecclesiastes 5:1-2** provides a frightening warning, "Walk prudently when you go to the house of God; and draw near to hear rather than to give the sacrifice of fools, for they

17

do not know that they do evil. Do not be rash with your mouth, and let not your heart utter anything hastily before God. For God is in heaven, and you on earth. Therefore let your words be few."

Prayer needs careful thought and prudent preparation. Otherwise, we will be offering the sacrifice of fools, performing evil and not even know it. Prayer is serious business. It is not a toy. It is not chit-chatting with a neighbor over coffee.

If John's disciples had to be taught to pray and Jesus' disciples had to be taught to pray, it stands to reason we have to be taught to pray. We cannot just continue doing whatever comes naturally.

We Must Desire To Learn

I am intrigued that Jesus waited until He was asked by the disciples to teach them to pray. In my finite wisdom, I would think that should have been on the short list of workshops with which to start the disciples' three-year training.

But Jesus waited until they asked. I can only gather that Jesus understood something perhaps I have not. Before people will learn anything, they have to want to.

If we are going to learn to pray, we have to want to. Do you want to learn?

The Lord Teaches Us

The disciples knew to whom they should go for this learning. John had taught his disciples to pray. Some of these men had been John's disciples and gone through his course on prayer.

However, in the presence of Jesus, they knew they had more to learn. They were not satisfied with just any training in prayer. They wanted the Lord's training.

We must have that same attitude. Even as we use a book such as this one, we must recognize that men cannot teach us to pray properly. Rather, we must go to the Lord and get His teaching. How can we do that? By going to His word. My prayer is that nothing in this book will be my own thinking, but simply a compilation of what the Bible says about prayer.

Make it a habit to notice Bible prayers. Look at the attitudes of proper prayer. Look at the habits of praying saints. Consider the ways in which God was addressed. Notice the praises and thanks given. Pay attention to the pleas made and intercessions offered. Give heed to the confessions uttered. Take special notice of the foundation and basis of their prayers.

A great resource is Herbert Lockyer's ***All The Prayers Of The Bible***. I cannot place my stamp of approval on everything he says about prayer, but his book provides a thorough compilation of Bible prayers.

Not Just a "How To" Course

I do not remember who I first heard make this point, but it changed my ideas about learning to pray forever. When addressing the request, he pointed out that the disciples did not just ask for a "how to" course. They wanted to be taught to pray.

Can you see the difference? The first is a matter of knowledge. The second is a matter of action.

Consider this, if you were pulled from a lake unconscious, who would you prefer to have by your side—someone who is an expert in how to perform CPR or someone who actually performs it?

19

In like manner, God is not interested in having Christians who know how to pray, are experts in prayer or can even teach the mechanics of prayer. He wants His children to pray. He wants me to pray. He wants you to pray.

Thank the Holy Spirit

What are we to do? We do not know how to pray, yet we know we must. **Romans 8:26-27** provides the answer to our dilemma. The Holy Spirit "helps in our weaknesses. For we do not know what we should pray for as we ought, but the Spirit Himself makes intercession for us."

We must not be complacent, thinking we can pray in whatever way we desire. Rather, we must grow in our prayer ability. At the same time, we must not wait until we know it all. We must start now; the Holy Spirit will take care of the rest.

Perhaps you have picked up this book to help you learn to pray. Do not wait until you have finished this book or any other to take your first step into the world of prayer. Pray right now. Do not read any further. Do not work through the challenges. Do not read my written prayer below. Pray for yourself right now. You are certain not to pray with complete propriety, but if you are God's child, the Holy Spirit will intercede for you in your weakness.

Have you prayed yet? If not, stop reading—pray now. If you did, congratulations. You are on your way to become a Praying Warrior.

Prayer Challenge:

Consider the model prayer in **Luke 11:2-4**. In your own words, list what Jesus did in this prayer.

He acknowledged the Father

Still having trouble praying? It usually helps to start with a good outline. Allow me to share two possible outlines you can use to help or make up your own. Fill in things you can pray for in the blanks and then pray through the prayers you have created.

ACTS

Adoration:

Confession:

Thanksgiving:

Supplication:

Finish the sentence[1]

Dear God, You are…

---

[1] This outline was adapted from the Our Spiritual Heritage Bible Class Curriculum, www.ourspiritualheritage.com.

21

Dear God, You…

Dear God, thank You for…

Dear God, forgive me for…

Dear God, help by…

Plug In:

Father in heaven,

Thank You for allowing me the avenue of prayer. Your grace is overwhelming.

I do not always know how to pray, what to say or how to say it in prayer. Please, accept my offerings and teach me to pray.

Thank You for allowing Your Holy Spirit to intercede for me.

I love You, Father.

In Your Son's name I pray,

Amen

Chapter 3

The Habit of Prayer

Pray Without Ceasing

"Rejoice always, pray without ceasing, in everything give thanks; for this is the will of God in Christ Jesus for you" (**I Thessalonians 5:16-18**).

The first time I read this passage, it conjured up images of monasteries. There we all were, walking around in sackcloth, our hands together, eyes closed (don't ask me how we were supposed to be walking around with our eyes closed), mumbling prayers under our breath unendingly. The "amen" was never heard because we were supposed to pray without ceasing, right?

A preacher once tried to explain this to me. He said this passage did not mean we literally prayed constantly. Rather, it meant we had a constant attitude of prayer and an unending prayer mindset.

I nodded my head and said, "Oh, that clears it all up."

Not really, but I wanted to sound spiritual. My real thought was, "What on earth are an attitude of prayer and a prayer mindset? Do I have either of those? If not, how do I get them?"

Gratefully, I have learned Paul was not trying to push us to grasp some ethereal attitude of prayer or a mystical prayer mindset. Rather, Paul was using a very common figure of speech called hyperbole, which is exaggeration.

We use this figure of speech all the time. (In case you didn't know it, I just used it.) It works like this. Someone asks you if you like to listen to a particular kind of music and you respond, "Oh yeah, I love that music. I listen to it *all the time.*"

Did you mean you listen to that music 24 hours a day, 7 days a week, 365 days a year? Did you mean you sneak your mp3 player to school, work and even the assembly so you can listen "without ceasing?" Of course not. You meant you listen frequently. You listen habitually. Further, you are not going to stop your frequent and habitual listening any time soon.

That is exactly what Paul meant. He used this figure three times in **I Thessalonians 5:16-18.** He said we should rejoice *always.* We should pray *without ceasing.* We should give thanks *in everything.* If someone asks us, "Do you ever pray?" We ought to be able to reply. "Oh yeah, I love to pray. I pray all the time."

Prayer must be an integral part of our lives. We must "rejoice always." That is, we are to pray habitually, frequently and consistently. We must "pray without ceasing." That is, our habit must never stop. We must give thanks "in everything." That is, we should pray as a response to every circumstance in our lives. Prayer should be in every aspect of our lives—whether home, school, work or church.

Daniel's Prayer Habit

One of the greatest Bible examples of a prayer habit is the Old Testament hero Daniel. Daniel's fellow governors and satraps did not like him very much. Frankly, little "Mr. Goody-Goody" was making them look bad. They had to do something to get him out of their way.

They knew Daniel prayed habitually. They were certain he would pray without ceasing. Therefore, they concocted a plan and convinced the king to make it illegal to pray to any god other than the king.

Foolishly, King Darius agreed. Was Daniel deterred? Not in the slightest. **Daniel 6:10** says, "When Daniel knew that the writing was signed, he went home. And in his upper room, with his windows open toward Jerusalem, he knelt down on his knees three times that day, and prayed and gave thanks before his God, as was his custom since early days."

Daniel had a hefty prayer habit. Even the king's decree could not break it. Daniel prayed without ceasing. He prayed all the time.

A huge part of praying without ceasing is having a prayer custom. Daniel's prayer custom was to pray three times a day. We should follow his example, having a scheduled prayer habit with which we follow through no matter what. If we develop that habit in good times, it will be easier to maintain in bad.

Nehemiah's Prayer Habit

Another great habitual prayer is Nehemiah, the Old Testament cupbearer who became governor of Judah and led the people to rebuild Jerusalem's walls. Throughout **Nehemiah**, we read his prayers.

When Hanani told him of the still ruined wall in Jerusalem, he prayed. "So it was, when I heard these words, that I sat down and wept, and mourned for many days; I was fasting and praying before the God of heaven" (**Nehemiah 1:4**).

When Artaxerxes asked Nehemiah to explain his sadness, he wrote, "So I prayed to the God of heaven…" (**Nehemiah 2:4**).

Nehemiah prayed in response to taunting enemies. "Hear, O our God, for we are despised; turn their reproach on their own heads, and give them as plunder to a land of captivity! Do not cover their iniquity, and do not let their sin be blotted out from before You; for they have provoked You to anger before the builders" (**Nehemiah 4:4-5**).

He prayed for strengthening as the enemies declared his hands to be weak. "For they all were trying to make us afraid, saying 'Their hands will be weakened in the work, and it will not be done.' Now therefore, o God, strengthen my hands" (**Nehemiah 6:9**).

He even prayed while he wrote his book, writing some of his prayers into it. For example, "Remember me, my God, for good according to all that I have done for this people" (**Nehemiah 5:19**). Also "My God, remember Tobiah and Sanballat, according to these their works and the prophetess Noadiah and the rest of the prophets who would have made me afraid" (**Nehemiah 6:14**).

Nehemiah prayed without ceasing. Under every circumstance he prayed. At times he prayed for days. At times he uttered quick momentary prayers. Whatever he was facing, whatever he was doing, prayer was part of it.

If we are going to pray without ceasing, we have to pray like this. Not just praying at set scheduled times, but also praying at a moment's notice because prayer is what is needed in that moment.

Jesus' Prayer Habit

The greatest example of an unbreakable prayer habit is Jesus. Jesus prayed all the time.

In **Mark 1:35**, He rose early to pray. "Now in the morning, having risen a long while before daylight, he went out and departed to a solitary place; and there He prayed." In **Matthew 14:23**, He prayed in the evening. "And when he had sent the multitudes away, He went up on the mountain by Himself to pray. Now when evening came, He was alone there." Prayer was a part of His daily devotion, His work and part of His plan for renewal following a long day's work.

In **Luke 6:12**, He prayed in preparation for a major decision, praying all night before He chose His apostles. "Now it came to pass in those days that He went out to the mountain to pray, and continued all night in prayer to God."

In **John 17**, we read of Jesus' great intercessory prayer for His 12 disciples and, in fact, for all believers, including us. "I pray for them. I do not pray for the world but for those whom You have given Me, for they are Yours...I do not pray for these alone, but also for those who will believe in Me through their word; that they all may be one" (**John 17:9, 20-21**).

In **Matthew 26:39**, He prayed in the face of suffering. "O My Father, if it is possible, let this cup pass from Me; nevertheless, not as I will, but as You will."

Jesus prayed all the time. If Jesus, God the Son in the flesh, needed the unbreakable habit of prayer communion with the Father, how much more do we need to pray all the time?

Our Prayer Habit

All of this is moot unless we bring it home to our lives. What kind of prayer habits do we have? Do we have any scheduled times of prayer? Daniel's example of three prayers a day is not binding. Mature Christianity does not equal having three scheduled prayer times per day. However, we do need to have some kind of prayer schedule.

What is your prayer schedule? If you do not have one, develop one. Are there times in your day that lend themselves to prayer? Some like to start their day off with prayer. Some like to end it that way. Some do both. Some close their office door at lunch time and pray. I've known people to take a morning walk and use that time to pray every day. I've known others to use their daily shower as prayer time. Only you can decide what your prayer habit is to be. You, however, must decide.

Further, you must keep your eyes open for those moments in which prayer is the right thing to do. Perhaps someone has told you of a struggle they are facing and you need to pray that God strengthen them. Perhaps someone just pulled out in front of you on the road and you need to pray for that driver to be safer and pay more attention. Or perhaps you need to pray to get your temper under control. Perhaps you have heard a rumor spreading about you and you need to pray for strength to do what is right and pray blessings upon your enemies. Whatever the case may be, you need to pay attention and pray, when prayer is what is necessary.

Prayer Challenge:

What is your prayer custom? Do you have one? If not, plan one below. How many times per day will you pray? When will you pray? Schedule it below and then follow through.

Review the past week, can you think of any times where prayer was needed? List them below.

Consider some situations you repeatedly encounter that warrant immediate prayer. List them below and be prepared to pray when they come up.

Plug In:

Father in heaven,

Please forgive me for the times in which I have ceased from prayer.

Thank You for the Bible examples You have provided of prayer. Strengthen me to be disciplined in prayer like Daniel, Nehemiah and Your Son, Jesus.

Please keep my eyes open to opportunities to pray to You throughout today and the week to come. Help me always turn to You in the face of every situation and in every aspect of my life.

Thank You for listening to me no matter when I pray.

I love You.

In Jesus' name I pray,

Amen

Chapter 4

Prayer: Ritual Or Response

Let's Be Careful Here

While in college, I attended a special series on prayer. Regrettably, my maturity level was so low at the time I do not remember much of what was said. About all I remember is how upset a friend of mine got over one point in the series. The preacher encouraged us to read from the scriptures while praying if we were not sure how to word our praises or requests. My friend thought that was the silliest thing he ever heard. After all, God wrote the Bible. He does not need us to quote it to Him. At the time, with all the logic and maturity an 18-year-old could muster, I agreed with my friend. Besides prayer should be from the heart, not from a book—right?

Sometime later I studied **Acts 4:24-30**. The apostles prayed, quoting from **Psalm 2**. I also studied Jesus' crucifixion. In **Luke 23:46**, when Jesus called on the Father, "Father, into Your hands I commit my spirit," He quoted **Psalm 31:5**. In **Matthew 27:46**, when Jesus prayed, "My God, My God, why have You forsaken Me", He quoted **Psalm 22:1**.

In the same vein, I have heard Christians mock written prayers others might repeat in certain situations. In fact, I have at times been chief among those who criticized others for having a book of prayers. Again, prayer should come from the heart, not from a book.

Then I began to notice how many songs addressed to God I have repeatedly sung and how many end with "Amen." Then it occurred to me—these are written and repeated prayers. Some of which I repeat on my own in certain circumstances. Is my hymn book a book of prayers? To some extent, yes.

How painful it was to be skewered by my own sword. I have to admit that quoting scripture in prayer and even reading and repeating a prayer are legitimate. Whew! I am glad to get that off my chest.

Why am I telling you this? Because I want you to fully understand what this chapter is truly about. Its title is "Prayer: Ritual or Response." While prayer is to be habitual, it must never become a ritual. Prayer is always to be a response from the heart to God. However, the issue is not about where the words originate. What is the issue then?

Pray In Spirit and Truth

The answer can be found in **John 4:24**. We are to worship in spirit and truth. That means we are to pray in spirit and truth.

Praying in truth includes praying according to God's revealed truth, praying sincerely, praying what is truth, etc. Praying in spirit means the prayer is not about gratifying the flesh. Further, it means more than just the flesh is involved in the prayer. Our entire spirit, the very center of our being must be involved. Our heart must be involved.

Reading a prayer from a book can easily become ritualistic, especially if we repeat it so much we are not even thinking about what we are really praying anymore. For that matter, so can singing all those songs from a book. Quoting Scripture in prayer may also mean we are not thinking about what we are saying, but not necessarily.

Who could deny Jesus was praying from the heart when He cried, "My God, My God why have You forsaken Me?" It simply happened that the words of **Psalm 22** mirrored the cry of Jesus' heart.

Have you ever had a time when your mouth was moving in prayer, but nothing was going on in your heart? I recall a night when it struck me that I was nearly 20 years old, thinking of devoting myself to preaching and yet my nightly prayers always came out the same. I could say them in my sleep (and often did). "Dear God, thank you for today and the many blessings you have given me. Please, forgive me of my sins and help me not to sin tomorrow. Please help me sleep well. In Jesus name I pray, Amen." I know, I know, you are staggered by the depth and profound nature of my vain repetition.

Why was that vain repetition? Not because I said the same thing each night. There are times to repeat prayers. These were vain repetitions because I was not responding to God—I was going through the motions. My parents taught me from childhood to say my "night-night" prayers. That is all I was doing. I came up with these words all on my own. But, they were no more than a nightly ritual.

Responding To God

In the Bible, whether the prayer was quoting Scripture or not, it was always a response from a believer's heart to God. It was always prompted by something He did, something He could do or something about His character.

How many times can we find the psalmist saying he will praise God because of His marvelous works? Consider **Psalm 9:1** for example, "I will praise You, O Lord with my whole heart; I will tell of all Your marvelous works." When David praised God it was not just because God said so. He was responding to the great work of God.

In like manner, the elders in **Revelation 4-5** were responding from the heart to God's power, holiness and mercy. "You are worthy, O Lord, to receive glory and honor and power; for you created all things, and by Your will they exist and were created...Blessing and honor and glory and power be to Him who sits on the throne, and to the Lamb, forever and ever!" (**Revelation 4:11; 5:13**).

In **Psalm 118:1, 29**, why was the psalmist thankful? Not because he knew he had to mark "thanksgiving" off his daily religion checklist. His thanksgiving was a response to God's greatness. "Oh give thanks to the Lord, for He is good! For His mercy endures forever."

Why did Asaph cry out to God in **Psalm 77**? Because God had what Asaph needed; strength, salvation and deliverance. "Your way, O God, is in the sanctuary; who is so great a God as our God? You are the God who does wonders; You have declared Your strength among the peoples. You have with Your arm redeemed Your people" (**Psalm 77:13-15**). Asaph was responding from the heart to God's lovingkindness and power.

In **Luke 18:13**, the publican's confession was clearly a heartfelt response. "God, be merciful to me a sinner!" This tax collector responded to God's holiness with confession. He responded to God's mercy with a request for forgiveness.

Are our prayers simply a ritual? Are we going through the motions because we have been taught prayer is an act of worship? Or are our prayers a response to God from the heart? This issue is not what is being said or who developed the words being said. The issue is what motivates the prayer.

Are we awed by God; and, therefore, praise Him? Are we overjoyed at His goodness; and, therefore, thank Him? Are we humbled by His holiness; and, therefore, confess to Him? Are we amazed by His might; and, therefore, make requests of Him? Or are we just doing what Mom and Dad taught us—our nightly religious duty?

Prayer is to be our response to God. This is why Bible study should be connected to prayer. How can we respond to God if we do not know Him through His word?

In **Mark 12:24**, Jesus connected knowing the scriptures with knowing God when He rebuked the Sadducees, saying, "Are you not therefore mistaken, because you do not know the Scriptures nor the power of God?" If we do not know the scriptures, we will not know the power of God or anything else about Him.

When we read the stories of His greatness, His power, His holiness and His mercy, we get to know God. As we learn to know God, we, like all those we have mentioned as examples in this chapter, will be led to pray. We will be led to respond from the heart to God, because we know that is what He deserves. "You are worthy, O Lord."

Prayer Challenge:

Read through Bible books like **Daniel** or **Nehemiah**, in which we find several prayers. Why did these men pray? How were their prayers a response to God and not just a ritual of prayer?

What is it about God that causes you to pray?

Plug In:

Our Father in Heaven,

Hallowed be Your name. Your mercy endures forever, therefore I give thanks to You.

I praise You for Your great power and might. Most of all I praise and thank You for Your great mercy and grace. You are worthy, O Lord, to receive glory and honor and power. Blessing, strength and wisdom are Yours.

Father, I acknowledge my transgressions. My sin is always before me. Against You, You only, I have sinned. That You are blameless when You judge. Please, wash me and I shall be whiter than snow. Create in me a clean heart, O God, and re-new a steadfast spirit within me.

Yours is the kingdom and the power and the glory forever.

I love You.

In Jesus' name,

Amen

aug 24 2022

Plugged In: High Voltage Prayer

Chapter 5

Talking To The Unseen God

A Visible God

Have you ever wondered why the Israelites had so much trouble with idolatry? We almost cannot read a page of Old Testament history without seeing God's nation turn its back on Him for a lump of gold or stick of wood.

One major attraction was the visibility of idols. Perhaps the most well-known example of idolatrous rebellion is the golden calf incident recorded in **Exodus 32**. Why did the Israelites want the calf? Because they could not see God. They wanted Aaron to make "gods that shall go before us" (**vs. 1**). That is, they wanted a god they could see leading the way.

Moses had been their visible connection to the invisible God, but he had disappeared on the mountain. With him gone, they wanted something tangible. Big mistake.

Regrettably, we can have the same problem. We want to see God and if we cannot see Him, we would at least like some kind of visible representation to help us focus our minds. Wondering how we can pray to the invisible God, we may not pray at all. After all, how do we talk to someone we cannot see?

The writer of **Hebrews** tells us one of Moses' great qualities was his ability to see "Him who is invisible" (**Hebrews 11:27**). Yet, even he wanted to literally see God. In **Exodus 33:18**, Moses requested, "Please, show me Your glory."

I am at a roadblock here. I want to be able to tell you how to see God. I want to be able to make this problem disappear and God appear. But I cannot. **I Timothy 1:17** explains that our King is not only eternal, immortal and alone wise. He is also invisible. I can do nothing to change that.

Why Invisible?

Why will God not let us see Him? God explained His reason for remaining invisible to Moses in **Exodus 33:20**: "You cannot see My face; for no man shall see Me, and live." In our weak humanity, we cannot survive the pure sight of God in all His glory. He maintains invisibility to help us, not to hinder prayer.

That probably makes sense to most of us. However, why not at least give us an image to hold in our minds, if not our hands, to facilitate prayer? I believe He has important reasons for this.

God is clearly opposed to physical representations and even mental images. In fact, that opposition was the purpose of the second commandment in **Exodus 20:4-6**:

You shall not make for yourself a carved image—any like-
ness of anything that is in heaven above, or that is in the
earth beneath, or that is in the water under the earth; you
shall not bow down to them nor serve them. For I, the Lord
Your God, am a jealous God, visiting the iniquity of the fa-
thers upon the children to the third and fourth generations of
those who hate Me, but showing mercy to thousands, to
those who love Me and keep My commandments.

This commandment was not a repeat of the first, "You shall
have no other gods before Me" (**Exodus 20:3**). These two
commandments taught the Israelites to worship only Jehovah
God and never worship Jehovah by developing an image to
represent Him.

But why? Surely an image that helps us focus our thoughts
toward God cannot be all that bad. Or could it?

If we did develop some image of God, what would it be?
Here we are, the finite, limited in our imagination by what we
have seen, trying to develop an image of the infinite? What
would it be?

Could we do better than the Israelites who made a golden
calf? Could we do better than ancient pagans, whose images
were mere variations on man and animals? In **Romans 1:22-
23**, God said those who did this professed to be wise, but were
fools. They traded the God of glory for something corruptible.

No matter what we envision in our mind's eye, draw on
paper or mold with gold, our image will be trading what God
really is for something less. Even worse, when we fix that image in our minds, our understanding of God will become limited by our picture. We may picture Him as an extremely powerful bull with many eyes to see all, many legs to go everywhere and many horns to have great power, but He will become to us nothing more than a variation on a cow.

Examine the pagans and their gods. Though more powerful,
they were nothing more than glorified humans, with the same

flaws and faults. They were fickle, impetuous, prone to error and even guilty of sin. We must never have that view of Jehovah.

Any image we create will have problems. How can the finite represent the infinite? How can the created represent the self-existent? How can the corruptible represent the incorruptible? How can the temporal represent the eternal? How can the dying represent the immortal? How can the confined represent the omnipresent?

It cannot be done; we must not even try.

Walking By Faith, Not By Sight

I am sorry to have been of so little help. Perhaps, however, understanding why it must be this way will help of itself.

Nevertheless, as we consider praying to the unseen God there is one area of great help—faith. Remember **II Corinthians 5:7**: "We walk by faith, not by sight." According to **Hebrews 11:1**, "Faith is the substance of things hoped for, the evidence of things not seen."

God wants this faith from us. He wants conviction and surrender to the evidence He has given. He does not want us to base our devotion on what we have seen of Him or our lack of faith on what we cannot see.

Do not misunderstand; our faith is not blind. We have visible evidence upon which we may base intelligent faith. **Romans 1:20** highlights this when Paul claimed God's invisible attributes are declared through His creative work. Further, the Scripture itself provides evidences to convince us, producing faith (**Romans 10:17**). In the end, however, we cannot see God as we see each other. Our conviction then is faith and not sight.

If we need help praying to the unseen God, we must increase our faith. If we want to increase our faith, we must get into God's word. We can read about the ancient prayer heroes. None of them ever saw God, but their prayers were amazing. We can read about and get to know Jesus through the word. In **John 14:9-11**, Jesus said if we get to know Him, we will know the Father.

Finally, and most importantly, we must remember even though we cannot see God and cannot feel Him, He is still there. David knew no matter where he went, God was with him: "Where can I go from Your Spirit? Or where can I flee from your presence" (**Psalm 139:7**). Remember the promise of **Hebrews 13:5**: "For he Himself has said, 'I will never leave you nor forsake you.'" God is with us right now. We must not forget it.

Prayer Challenge:

Read **Genesis 1-2** and give thought to the creation around you. List, in your own words, the invisible attributes of God to which Paul referred in **Romans 1:20**. Be as specific as you can.

What do you know about God that cannot be represented by any image we can imagine? Ponder the infinity of God today.

Plug In:

Father in heaven,

I cannot possibly imagine Your goodness, power and eternal nature. You are infinite and I am finite. Father, thank You for bestowing Your infinite mercy on me, a finite sinner.

Lord, I believe; please help my unbelief, forgiving me for those times when I have limited You with my own imagination. Strengthen my faith that I may see the unseen.

Abide with me, Father. Thank You for always being with me.

I love You.

In Jesus' name I pray,

Amen

Plugged In: High Voltage Prayer

Group Discussion:

What were the most important lessons you learned about prayer this week?

How did this week's readings help your prayer life?

What advice would you give others based on this week's reading to help them pray?

With what issues do you need help or prayers based on this week's reading?

Why is prayer one of the most important part of the Christian soldier's life?

How can we increase our desire to pray?

What is the key to being devoted to prayer?

What is it about God that causes us to need and want to pray to Him?

How do you overcome the inability to see God in your prayer life?

Plugged In: High Voltage Prayer

WEEK TWO

"Holy, holy, holy, Lord God Almighty, who was and is and is to come!...You are worthy, O Lord, to receive glory and honor and power; for You created all things and by Your will they exist and were created."

Revelation 4:8b, 11

Plugged In: High Voltage Prayer

Chapter 6

Prostrate in the Presence of the Holy

Unapproachable Light

Since our concept of holiness is limited by experience, we cannot fathom the holiness of God. The most holy among us have chinks in their armor and we have been disappointed by them time and again. Therefore, it is impossible to imagine absolute, complete, undefiled purity and holiness.

Even Scripture does not provide an exact description of God's perfect holiness. The Bible exclaims God's purity, and with almost crushing weight it repeatedly contrasts our complete and utter destitution due to sin and His absolute and perfect purity.

However, when we attempt to explain God's holiness, either from our own vocabulary or from scripture, we consistently come up short. As we asked in the previous chapter, how can finite human language describe the infinite God? The Scripture does, however, illustrate God's holiness as light.

I John 1:5 says, "God is light and in Him is no darkness at all." **James 1:17** describes God as "the Father of lights, with whom there is no variation or shadow of turning." Paul told Timothy that God dwells in "unapproachable light" (**I Timothy 6:16**).

Can you imagine dazzlingly brilliant, blinding light? Light in which is no darkness, not even a shadow? There is no safe place to look—no matter which direction you look or turn there is no shade or protection from the brilliance. Closing your eyes does not protect you because the light is so strong it cuts through your lids. It is so powerful even your own body casts no shadow.

Everything is exposed and bare in the presence of God's holy light. In fact, the only dark spot in this scene is us—the darkness we contain in our hearts because of sin and the times we have tried to hide from God's light.

Approaching the Unapproachable

How are we supposed to pray to this holy God? I don't know about you…actually, I do know about you. We are both sinners. Darkness has filled our hearts. Perhaps we have had moments, even days, of light. But we are just black spots in comparison to God's holiness.

We have to come to grips with this aspect of prayer. God is holy and we are not. We cannot produce even one shred of support for entering God's presence. Nevertheless, that is exactly what the holy God allows. Not only does He allow it, He allows it freely, any time we want.

Do you remember the story of Esther? In **Esther 3** Haman convinced King Ahasuerus to destroy all the Jews. In **Esther 4** Mordecai sent messages to his cousin Esther, the Queen. He wanted her to plead before the King on the Jews' behalf.

She responded in **Esther 4:11**:

All the king's servants and the people of the king's provinces know that any man or woman who goes into the inner court to the king, who has not been called, he has but one law: put all to death, except the one to whom the king holds out the golden scepter, that he may live. Yet I myself have not been called to go in to the king these thirty days.

We might expect God to have a similar system to deal with the unholy rabble that fills this world—to deal with us.

Can you imagine what it might be like? Wanting to praise God or thank Him, but knowing that approaching Him might end in death? Never would we think of prostrating ourselves to ask for something, even something as important and necessary as forgiveness. The most we could hope for is that He might call us into His presence.

But, of course, that is exactly what He has done. He has asked us to come into His presence. What an awesome God we have!

Only One Talent

We need to take seriously the warning from the parable of the talents in **Matthew 25:14-30**. The one-talent man recognized his master's holiness. He saw how hard, demanding and exacting such holiness was. Because of that, he was paralyzed by fear. When he was finally called into his master's presence, he had done nothing and could only give back the talent with which he started. The master rebuked him: "You wicked and lazy servant" (**Matthew 25:26**).

This parable is not about prayer. However, we might have the same problem with praying. When we look at the filthiness of our sins and the holiness of God, we might become paralyzed by fear saying, "How can we pray to a holy God?" Isaiah expressed this fear in **Isaiah 6:5**, "Woe is me, for I am undone! Because I am a man of unclean lips, and I dwell in the midst of a people of unclean lips."

In fact, we might refrain from prayer for this very reason. The master's response to the one talent man, though, should encourage us to approach God anyway. "You knew that I reap where I have not sown, and gather where I have not scattered seed. So you ought to have deposited my money with the bankers, and at my coming I would have received back my own with interest" (**Matthew 25:26-27**).

Do you get the point? The servant knew what a demanding and exacting master he had; he ought to have at least done something. That is what God expects of us. We are unholy. We have nothing to offer God. But instead of hiding until He demands our presence, we ought to at least pray something.

Again, we recall the Holy Spirit helps us in our weaknesses. When we do not know how to pray as we ought because we lack holiness, the Holy Spirit intercedes for us (**Romans 8:26-27**).

Please do not misunderstand. I am not saying the Lord wants us to come into His presence if we are living in rebellious sin. We will address that point in a later chapter. The point is that despite our sin and God's holiness, He still wants us to pray. How awesome is that?!

Prayer Challenge:

Think about God's holiness. What do you think that means about how we should approach God in prayer? With what attitudes should we pray?

Read **Psalms 29, 96** and **99**, psalms speaking of God's holiness. List the responses these psalms claim we should have to God's holiness.

Plug In:

Holy Father in heaven,

You, who dwell in Your holy heaven are great and greatly to be praised. The earth and all it contains rejoices in Your holiness.

Please be merciful to me, a sinner. Forgive my iniquities and cleanse me that I may have the holiness that comes from Your grace through faith in Your Holy Son.

If in anything I am regarding iniquity in my heart, please, open my eyes through Your word. Straighten my paths that I may be holy as You are holy.

Father, I praise and thank You that You allow my lowly offering of prayer.

I love You.

In Jesus' holy name I pray,

Amen

Chapter 7

Praying to the Almighty God

Even God Can't Do That

The situation was bleak. Ben-Hadad, king of Syria, had besieged Samaria. There was no food anywhere. It was so bad some of the people were turning to cannibalism, eating their own children. The king blamed God for this and decided to punish God's messenger. When he came to seize Elisha, however, the man of God explained that on the following day there would be plenty of food.

Then one of the king's assisting officers uttered some of the most regrettable words ever spoken: "Look, if the Lord would make windows in heaven, could this thing be?"

In essence, he said, "Wake up, Elisha. Even God can't do that."

Elisha responded, "You shall see it with your eyes, but you shall not eat of it."

That night, four lepers decided to seek mercy from the Syrians. They figured the Syrians might be gracious. If not, they would kill them quickly, which would be better than starving to death. When they got to the camp, however, they discovered the Syrians had fled, leaving in such a hurry that their provisions were still in the camp.

God had caused the Syrians to hear a noise of chariots. They thought Israel had hired help to mount a surprise attack and they fled in fear. There was all that food left for the Israelites. The lepers informed the king and Israel was saved.

The Israelites stormed the camp to get the plunder. However, the officer who had smarted off to Elisha was trampled to death by the people before he got even a single bite (**II Kings 6-7**).

Never say God can't.

The Power of God

Too often, I have tried to stress how powerful prayer is. I stressed prayer's power to get Christians to pray. While my heart was in the right place, I have learned my teaching was not. I got it wrong. Prayer has no power. I know that statement is shocking. Let me repeat it. Prayer has no power. God has all the power. Prayer is our means to plug in to God's power.

Ephesians 3:20 says, "Now to Him who is able to do exceedingly abundantly above all that we ask or think, according to the power that works in us." God is so powerful He can do all we ask or think. Not only that, He can do above all we ask or think. Not only that, He can do abundantly above all we ask or think. Not only that, He can do exceedingly abundantly above all we ask or think.

Please notice, however, God will do all of this according to the power that works in us. That is, God's power will work through us, accomplishing more than we can ask. However, we must ask. We become the conduits of God's power in this world, but only when we plug in to His power through prayer. Through all of this, we must keep the proper perspective. We must not believe in the power of prayer. Rather, we must believe in the power of God and, therefore, pray.

Allow me to illustrate. Consider your bedside lamp. Does it contain any power on its own? Of course not. When it is by itself you can flip the switch on and off all you want and no light will ever shine. What happens when we add an extension cord? Does it have any power now? No. Even with the extension cord the lamp has no power. What happens, however, the moment we plug the cord into a power source? We can flip the switch and the light shines. Power courses through the lamp. We are lamps, lifeless and dark by ourselves. God is the power source, filled with potential energy, just waiting for us to connect and allow His power into our lives. Prayer is the extension cord that reaches out and connects to the real power. The cord itself is not the power. However, without the cord, we cannot access the power. That is why we must plug in.

Moses' prayers did not cause the plagues to come on Egypt or lifted them when Pharaoh begged. The God to whom Moses prayed did that (**Exodus 6-13**).

Elijah's prayers did not stop the rain in Israel, bring fire down to the altar or start the rain again. The God to whom he prayed accomplished that (**I Kings 17-18**).

Elisha's prayer did not bring the dead back to life. The God to whom he prayed performed that (**II Kings 4**).

One of the great problems we have with prayer is this mistaken notion that prayer is powerful. When we believe the power resides in prayer itself and forget that it actually resides in the God to whom we pray, we find ourselves asking, "I prayed, why didn't anything happen?"

However, when we remember the truth, we can remember that God, who is all-powerful, is not obligated by our prayers to do what we ask, no matter how badly we desire it or how fervently we pray for it. It is God's power to use or to withhold at His discretion.

Therefore, when we pray and things do not go our way, we do not say, "What went wrong? Prayer must not work." Rather, we remember we were praying to the all-powerful God. If He did not do what we asked, He must have had His reasons.

In a later chapter we will delve into the reasons God says, "No." In this chapter we just need to note the great power of God. Therefore, allow me to repeat, prayer is not powerful—God is!

Pulling God Out Of The Box

We must not limit God's power with our small thinking. I remember vividly when I learned how guilty we Christians can be of putting God in a box.

My family and I were visiting my hometown because of my dad's failing health. He had been diagnosed with pancreatic cancer four months earlier. Despite an early upswing, his health had gone downhill. We all knew his death was imminent if events followed their natural course.

Despite the state of my dad's health, I was willing to fight. I knew there would be no miracles of healing. I could not pray a prayer of recovery or lay healing hands on my dad. However, I was certain prayer connected me to the most powerful force in the universe. Jehovah God, if He chose, could turn things around. We were at a weeknight assembly of the congregation of which my parents were members. The brethren asked me to lead them in the dismissal prayer.

Despite its personal nature, about the only issue on my mind was my dad's health. Therefore, I used most of that prayer to ask for God's merciful hand to spare my dad's life and remove the cancer. Before leaving the building one well-meaning sister, who was only visiting, pulled my wife aside to get her to prepare me for reality. "God doesn't work miracles anymore. You need to help him get ready for his dad's death."

I know you expect me to tell you God worked in mysterious ways and my father lived for years because of my prayer. God did not work that way. Instead, He said no to my prayer; my dad died within two days. Was the visiting sister right after all? No. That week, I was not nearly so upset that God denied my request. I was already no stranger to death. I understood how the world works. God cannot say yes to every request on behalf of dying loved ones. However, I was upset that my sister in Christ could not fathom a God powerful enough to turn my Dad's health around. I realized with our desire to be realistic, we sometimes place God in a box.

We are talking about the God who created the universe in six days just by speaking. We are talking about the God who parted the Red Sea. We are talking about the God who stores up the rain, snow and hail in storehouses that none can open. We are talking about the God who has set the boundaries of the nations. We are talking about the God who raises the dead. He can do anything.

Now that the Scripture has been confirmed, I believe God no longer uses miracles to reveal His word. But that does not mean God can do nothing. He can work in ways we cannot fathom. God is that powerful. We need to pray like God is the most powerful being in existence. Because He is.

Ephesians 3:20-21 reminds us God can do exceedingly abundantly beyond all we ask or think. Certainly, He reserves the right to say, "No." But He is still powerful enough to do more than the requests with which we can challenge Him.

Are there issues you have not taken to God in prayer because you believe He cannot do anything about them? If there are, then stop reading and take them to God in prayer right now.

Never say God can't. Sometimes He won't. But never say He can't.

Prayer Challenge:

Reflect on the examples of God's power detailed in the Bible. List some of the most powerful events you can remember below:

What do these events demonstrate about the power of God and His ability to handle or help with your requests?

Plug In:

Almighty God and Father,

You, who created the heavens and the earth, are worthy of praise, blessing, honor and glory.

Who can make crooked what You have straightened or straighten what You have made crooked? You have spoken and who can change it?

Please forgive me for the times I have denied Your power. I believe, help my unbelief. Strengthen and increase my faith that I may trust in Your power.

Give me understanding to live with Your will when you deny my requests. Help me trust that You know when to extend Your power and when to withhold it.

Thank You for extending Your power to conquer sin and death for me.

I love You.

In Jesus' name I pray,

Amen

Plugged In: High Voltage Prayer

Chapter 8

Informing the All-Knowing

What Can We Tell Him

We see the commercials every December. "What do you get the person who has everything?" Dramatic Pause "Something from our store."

Every day we face this same dilemma in prayer. What do we tell the God who knows everything? Read **Psalm 139:13-16**.

For You formed my inward parts; You covered me in my mother's womb. I will praise you, for I am fearfully and wonderfully made; marvelous are Your works, and that my soul knows very well. My frame was not hidden from You, when I was made in secret, and skillfully wrought in the lowest parts of the earth. Your eyes saw my substance, being yet unformed. And in Your book they all were written, the days fashioned for me, when as yet there were none of them.

Rest assured. God knows.

Yet, this knowledge often produces prayer-stopping questions. Why thank God if He already knows we are thankful? Why ask if He already knows what we need? Why confess sins if He already knows all the wrong things we have done? Why pray at all if God already knows what we are going to say and what He is going to do? Have you ever asked these kinds of questions?

More than a few Christians have killed their prayer lives with them.

Pray Anyway

Let me begin by saying whether we are ever satisfied with anyone's answers to these questions or not, we need to pray anyway. Don't you think Abraham knew that God knew? What about Moses? Mary? David? Deborah? Peter? Paul?

Let us not be so arrogant as to think we are the first saints to grapple with these deep issues. Yet these great servants of God were all people of prayer. Amazingly enough, they were so convinced these questions should not hinder us they never even dealt with them in scripture. Whatever answer we come up with regarding these questions, whether you are satisfied with my answers to these questions or not, the take away is the same—pray anyway.

No Surprises

In reality, instead of being a hindrance to prayer, God's omniscience ought to be a real boost to our prayer lives.

My parents always assured me they knew when I had done something bad. They knew because I would avoid talking to them. Why did I avoid them? I did not want them to know. I do not have to play that game with God. He already knows. There are no surprises between me and God.

He knows what is coming, but wants us to pray about it anyway. There is no confession that will shock Him into a stupor, saying, "Whoa, I don't know if I can forgive that one." There is no request that will stop Him in His tracks, saying, "Wow, I never thought anyone would ask for that." Further, we do not have to worry that God might say, "Boy, bad timing. If you had told me that last week, I might have done something about it. But I didn't see this one coming. Tough luck for you."

We are not a big shock to God. That is not to say we do not disappoint God at times. But God knew all of those times before we were here and sent His Son to die anyway. There are no surprises for God, so pray anyway.

God's Big Picture

I have read and reread and reread **James 5:16**. "The effective, fervent prayer of a righteous man avails much."

I have read the stories of Abraham talking to God about Sodom and Gomorrah (**Genesis 18:17-33**) and Moses interceding on behalf of Israel (**Exodus 32:11-14**). I just did not get it.

If God knows everything, then He already knew what was going to happen in each of these cases. If God already knew what was going to happen, then how can we say the prayers had any real effect? When I begin to think this way, frankly, I feel like prayer has no point. Yet, I have studied my Bible and I know prayer does have a point. What is that point?

Allow me to share three principles that have helped me deal with these questions.

First, prayer is not for God's benefit. It is for ours. The prayers of Abraham and Moses were not for God's benefit, but theirs. Therefore, the real importance of Abraham and Moses' prayers was not how it impacted God, but how it impacted them. The real importance of our prayer is not how it impacts God, but how it impacts us.

When I finally understood this, my whole view of these issues changed. In the moment this snapped into place, I recognized that whether or not God actually changed because of my prayers is not important. What is important is that I change because of my prayers. Despite our tendency to want to bend God to our will through prayer, we must learn prayer is actually the means by which God bends us to His will. That was important; remember it.

Second, prayer brings the finite in connection with the infinite. God's explanation of how our prayers impact Him is limited by our finite ability to understand His nature and work. As we have already stated, our finite language and mental imagery cannot accurately describe God or how He thinks and acts. Similarly, our finite language and mental imagery cannot accurately describe how God responds to or is impacted by our prayers.

When I grasped this principle (or actually recognized that I could not grasp this principle), I recognized that the passages in question were clearly not explaining the exact way our prayers impact God. They were written accommodatively to help us come as close to understanding how prayers impact God as we can get. That is, God used a figure of speech. It is called anthropopathism, attributing human passions, actions or attributes to God.

Third, when we struggle with how our prayers impact God, it is typically because we are thinking of God as nothing more than a super-powered human. We view Him as really powerful but still bound by the same laws of time and space as we are.

I am not trying to go Star Trek on you here, but we need to open our minds to the fact that God does not dwell within our "space-time continuum." God created time in the same way He created matter and energy. As the Creator, He is not bound by linear time in the way we are anymore than He is bound by the laws of matter and energy in the way we are.

If a request impacted us, we had one thought or plan in mind until we heard the request. Then we changed our thought or plan. In our limited minds, we think God must be impacted by our prayers in the same way, otherwise He was not impacted by them. That is, we believe He must have one thought in mind up to the point of our prayer. Then we pray. Then His mind changes. Otherwise, our prayer had no impact. It doesn't work that way.

Consider the picture below:

GOD

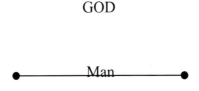

The line is the extent of time from Creation to Judgment. Man lives within the confines of linear time. We look back and see history. We imagine ahead and call it the future. Every moment leads to the next and we have little idea what a moment will bring until it happens.

God, however, exists outside the confines of linear time. He does not live from moment to moment. He has always seen the beginning, the end and everything in between. Every choice we make, every action we take and every prayer we utter has been in the mind of God for eternity. No, He did not plan our choices, our actions or our prayers. He simply knew what they would be from eternity.

Therefore, God's plans were not made at one point in time and then changed in the moment of a prayer. Rather, God's plans were made and set before the beginning with all of our actions and prayers in mind. Thus, without our actions and prayers, God would have acted in one way. However, because He was aware of our coming actions and prayers, He acts in a different way. Our prayers impacted His plans.

Whoa, am I glad that explanation is over with. If I did not just completely confuse you, perhaps this answer, which helps me, will help you as well.

However, if I did completely confuse you or if you think I have lost my mind, then please, just go back to the verses mentioned above and trust God. If He says our prayers avail much with Him, they do. That is all we need to know. Rest comfortably knowing you cannot surprise God and, therefore, pray to Him, even when you do not understand how it works.

Pray anyway.

Prayer Challenge:

Are there any sins you have been afraid to confess? God already knows them. Go ahead and confess them right now.

Are there any other prayers you haven't prayed because of God's omniscience? Pray them right now.

Read **Psalm 139**. How did David respond to God's omniscience?

Plug In:

All-knowing Father in heaven,

I stand in awe of You. Your infinite wisdom and knowledge astounds and even confuses me. But Father I am thankful that You know.

Father, thank You for sending Your Son despite knowing how sinful I was going to be.

Please grant me strength and increase my faith that I may trust Your infinite wisdom and knowledge.

Please grant me wisdom and understanding through the knowledge of Your Son.

I love You.

In Jesus' name I pray,

Amen

Plugged In: High Voltage Prayer

Chapter 9

Prayer in Every Place

God Is Everywhere

Ben-Hadad, king of Syria, was looking for a fight with Israel. Having goaded Ahab, he overconfidently sat back and waited. However, the Lord delivered Syria into the hand of Israel that day.

Then Ben-Hadad heeded the worst advice possible. In **I Kings 20:23-25**, he was told his army was defeated because Jehovah of Israel must be a god of the hills. If the Syrians fought Israel on the plains, they were sure to win. But they did not understand Jehovah.

God's anger was aroused. Despite Ahab's own wickedness, Jehovah wanted to demonstrate to the Gentile nation that He is not like the false gods. He is God in every place. In **I Kings 20:28**, God explained through his prophet that he would deliver Syria into Ahab's hand a second time:

> *Then a man of God came and spoke to the king of Israel, and said, "Thus says the Lord: 'Because the Syrians have said, "The Lord is God of the hills, but He is not God of the valleys," therefore I will deliver all this great multitude into your hand, and you shall know that I am the Lord.'"*

Ben-Hadad and the Syrians learned an important lesson about our God. He is God everywhere. What an important concept to grasp for our prayer lives. Jehovah is God everywhere. No matter where we are, we can pray to Him.

Jesus emphasized this while speaking with the Samaritan woman in **John 4:24**. She was concerned about the argument over which mountain was the proper place of worship. Jesus explained that God is spirit. He is not flesh and blood like us. He is not bound by time and space as we are.

What matters then is not where we pray but that we pray and how we pray.

We Cannot Hide

There are some frightening aspects to this side of God. If Jehovah is God everywhere, we cannot hide from Him anywhere. **Psalm 139:7** asks, "Where can I go from Your Spirit? Or where can I flee from Your presence?"

What does this mean for prayer? It means we cannot fake it. Let's face it, when it comes to the brethren, we can spend our week in sin and put on a good show on Sunday. Many times the brethren will never know. We can hide our sins from them. But not so with God. He was there when we gossiped the other day. He was there when we told that little white lie. When we looked at that woman to lust, God saw that too.

We cannot hide from God, so we might as well not try to hide anything from God. David described how his life went when he tried to hide his sins from God and how his life changed when he confessed in **Psalm 32:3-5**:

When I kept silent, my bones grew old through my groaning all the day long. For day and night Your hand was heavy upon me; my vitality was turned into the drought of summer. I acknowledged my sin to You, and my iniquity I have not hidden. I said, "I will confess my transgressions to the Lord," and You forgave the iniquity of my sin.

We Cannot Be Hidden

While we often look at the frightening side of **Psalm 139:7**, there is also a comforting side. Not only can we not hide from God, we cannot be hidden.

Consider the comfort of **Psalm 139:9-12**:

If I take the wings of morning, and dwell in the uttermost parts of the sea, even there Your hand shall lead me, and Your right hand shall hold me. If I say, "Surely the darkness shall fall on me," even the night shall be light about me; indeed, the darkness shall not hide from You, But the night shines as the day; the darkness and the light are both alike to You.

No matter what we are facing, no matter where we are, no matter what is happening around us, God is with us. We need only pray to Him.

God says to us, through **Hebrews 13:5-6**, "He Himself has said, 'I will never leave your nor forsake you.' So we may boldly say: 'The Lord is my helper; I will not fear. What can man do to me?'"

God never promised our lives would be easy and trouble free. He did promise, however, to be with us no matter what our lives held in store. We can pray to Him for guidance to take the way of escape from any temptation. We can pray to Him for wisdom to handle any situation properly. We can pray to Him for strength to do all things.

Consider Ezekiel in **Ezekiel 1**. Recently taken captive and carried thousands of miles from the temple where he would have served as a priest, Ezekiel surely felt separated from God. But in a vision, he learned even in captivity he was not hidden from God.

Consider the prayers of Daniel in **Daniel 6**. In a land far from home, while surrounded by those who sought his downfall, Daniel's prayers were heard. He was saved from the lion's den and from the plots of his co-workers. Even in the lion's den Daniel was not hidden from God.

Consider Jonah's prayer in **Jonah 2**. Jonah had been cast off a ship and swallowed by a great fish. For three days and nights he remained there but his prayers were heard and he was freed. More amazing is why he was there. Jonah had rebelled against God's plan and was being judged. When he repented, however, he prayed and God listened. Even in the belly of a great fish, in the bowels of the deep, while facing judgment for rebellion, the penitent Jonah was not hidden from God.

I do not know what fears you may be facing. I do not know what burdens you may be bearing. I do not know with what troubles you may be toiling. But I do know if you are God's child, He is with you.

As David said in **Psalm 139:8**, "If I ascend into heaven, You are there; If I make my bed in hell, behold You are there." There are days when life will be going so well you will feel as though you are already in heaven. In those days, it is easy to pray to God. There will also be days when you will feel as though you are making your bed in hell. Prayer may not come so easy on those days. Remember, nevertheless, God is still with you. You can still pray.

Even better, God wants you to pray because He cares for you:

> *Be anxious for nothing, but in everything by prayer and supplication, with thanksgiving, let your requests be made known to God, which surpasses all understanding, will guard your hearts and minds through Christ Jesus (**Philippians 4:6-7**).*

> *Therefore humble yourselves under the mighty hand of God, that He may exalt you in due time, casting all your care upon Him, for He cares for you (**I Peter 5:6-7**).*

Prayer Challenge:

List the places you go on a regular basis. God is there. What kind of prayers might be helpful in those places?

List some difficult places or times you have faced. What prayers helped you then or could help you if you ever find yourself there again?

Plug In:

Father in heaven,

Your power is to be greatly praised in every place.

Thank You for being with me at all times. I am so awed and comforted by Your ever-presence.

Father, I am sorry for the many times in which I let You down. I know You have seen them all.

Please forgive me and be merciful to me a sinner.

Abide with me Father and guide me through Your Word to please You in every place I go today.

I love You.

In Jesus' name I pray,

Amen

Chapter 10

Praying to the Loving Redeemer

God Is Love

What a powerful statement. God is love. Let us not get lost in the metaphor. God is a being, not an emotion. John was not trying to present Jehovah as the Greeks and Romans might present Artemis or Venus. God is not a physical representation of love. Nor is He the god of love. John's point in **I John 4:8, 16** is that God embodies in His existence and character all the attributes of love.

79

He who does not love does not know God, for God is love (vs. 8).

And we have known and believed the love that God has for us. God is love, and he who abides in love abides in God, and God in him (vs. 16).

We can read **I Corinthians 13:4-7** and learn that God suffers long with us. He is kind to us. He does not envy us. But neither does He parade Himself or puff Himself up. He does not behave rudely. He never seeks His own, but looks out for our best interests. He is not provoked. He does not think evil. He does not rejoice in iniquity but rejoices in the truth. He bears with us through all things. He believes all things. He hopes all things and He endures all things.

What a relief. The all-knowing, all-powerful, all-present, all-holy God is all-loving.

Though He has every right to squash us at the first sight of sin, He does not. Though He has every right to be provoked by our wickedness, He is not. Though He has all authority with which to humiliate us as He displays His power and worth, He has not.

God is love.

When John said God is love, he also explained how much we can trust God's love. God's love is dependent on His nature, not ours. God does not love us because of anything we are or have done. God does not love us because we are smart. He does not love us because we are pretty. He does not love us because we are clever and witty. He does not love us because we are good. He does not love us because we love Him. Rather He loves us because He is love. No matter how we might change. He never changes.

Since His love is not based on us, we cannot lose His love based on anything we do or have done. If we get in a car wreck and lose our good looks, God still loves us. If we grow old and lose our strength and ability, He still loves us. If we have a major stroke and lose our mental capabilities, He still loves us. If we sin and lose our relationship with Him, He still loves us, seeking us as the shepherd searches for his lost sheep. We can trust God to love us no matter what because God is love.

That is so refreshing. We do not have to try to win God's love as we do everyone else's. God has given it to us and continues to give it to us. God is love.

God So Loved

Perhaps the most well-known verse in the entire Bible is **John 3:16**: "For God so loved the world that He gave His only begotten Son, that whoever believes in Him should not perish but have everlasting life." God's love brought about our redemption.

Paul said we are "sold under sin" in **Romans 7:14**. **Ephesians 2:1** teaches that sin has killed us. As the dead, we can do nothing to affect our salvation. The proverbialist asked, "Who can say, 'I have made my heart clean, I am pure from my sin?'" (**Proverbs 20:9**). That is our sad situation. We are sinful and we cannot do anything about it.

Praise the Lord; He did something about it. He sent His Son, Jesus Christ, into the world to die. **I Peter 3:18** says: "For Christ also suffered once for sins, the just for the unjust, that he might bring us to God." Through this death, Jesus redeemed us. John explained God's love in **I John 4:9** saying:

> In this the love of God was manifested toward us, that God has sent His only begotten Son into the world, that we might live through Him. In this is love, not that we loved God, but that He loves us and sent His Son to be the propitiation for our sins.

God bought us back from our slavery to sin. **Galatians 4:3-5** explains:

Even so we, when we were children, were in bondage under the elements of the world. But when the fullness of the time had come, God sent forth His Son, born of a woman, born under the law, to redeem those who were under the law, that we might receive adoption as sons.

Paul drove this point home in **I Corinthians 6:20**, explaining what this means for us: "For you were bought at a price; therefore glorify God in your body and in your spirit, which are God's." We have been bought with a price. The amazing cost was Jesus' blood. Therefore we must glorify God with our body and our spirit.

This ought to affect our prayer life. When we constantly remember God is our redeemer and savior, how could we do anything but glorify Him, praise Him and honor Him? What a great deal we owe our loving God. Since we can never repay Him, we ought to spend a great deal of time thanking and praising Him. As David said in **Psalm 63:3**, "Because Your lovingkindness is better than life, my lips shall praise You."

Entrance Into His Gates

Up to this point, we have learned about the power and holiness of God. Through those chapters you may have felt the great paradox. God wants us to pray, in fact, commands us to pray. But how on earth can puny sinners like us come into the presence of the all-powerful and supremely holy God?

We can do so because He loves us.

In the world, we have seen people who regard themselves as holy and they have little love. Do you remember the priest and Levite from the famous parable of the Good Samaritan (**Luke 10:30-36**). They viewed themselves as very holy. Try to think like the priest and the Levite. Perhaps they thought the wounded man was unholy and had simply been judged by God. Who were they to interfere? Perhaps they were worried about having their own personal holiness defiled. If they helped the man and he died, they would become unclean and be refused from temple service. Whatever the case, their focus on holiness stopped their love.

In the world, we have seen people with great power. Instead of love, they display lordship. Jesus told of these in **Matthew 20:25**: "You know that the rulers of the Gentiles lord it over them, and those who are great exercise authority over them."

If God were like man, we would not dare pray to Him. But He is not. His holiness and His power do not deter His love. He is love.

Therefore as **Psalm 69:16** says, God hears our prayers because of His lovingkindness. In fact, because of His love and the redemption He has offered through Christ, we can boldly (not boastfully, brazenly or brashly) draw near to His presence in prayer:

*Therefore, brethren, having boldness to enter the Holiest by the blood of Jesus, by a new and living way which He consecrated for us, through the veil, that is, His flesh, and having a High Priest over the house of God, let us draw near with a true heart in full assurance of faith, having our hearts sprinkled from an evil conscience and our bodies washed with pure water (**Hebrews 10:19-22**).*

How awesome is that?

Wait On The Lord

Because of God's love, we can trust Him to do what is best for us. However, His best for us may not occur immediately. Too often we expect God to hear our prayer and do something right away. He does not always work that way. In fact, scripturally, many of His answers to prayer occurred over time. Because we know and trust God's love, we can pray and then wait on the Lord to do what is best in His time.

Psalm 40 is powerful. David was in the horrible pit. He said his feet were in miry clay. David's life was not free from trouble, as we know well. Some of his troubles were of his own making, but many were not.

While in trouble, he did not turn His back in anger against God; he trusted God. He waited on the Lord to bring him through trouble in the Lord's time. Because he prayed and waited on the Lord, he was able to praise God saying:

I waited patiently for the Lord; and He inclined to me, and heard my cry. He also brought me up out of a horrible pit, out of the miry clay, and set my feet upon a rock, and established my steps. He has put a new song in my mouth—Praise to our God; Many will see it and fear, and will trust in the Lord (Psalm 40:1-3).

Keep in mind the great patience of God's plan through Jesus. God worked His plan to bring Jesus over thousands of years from the time Adam and Eve first sinned. He did not immediately solve mankind's sin problem. Instead, He developed a plan that would be best for all involved and would work out in the fullness of His time.

The same is true in our lives. God will not immediately solve our problems. But He will take care of us. "All things work together for good for those who love God" (**Romans 8:28**).

Many times we may think God is late. However, God is always right on time. Because God is the loving redeemer, we can trust Him to take care of us. As **Psalm 30:5** says, "Weeping may endure for a night, but joy comes in the morning."

Prayer Challenge:

In **Psalm 63:3**, David said, "Because your lovingkindness is better than life, my lips shall praise you." List the ways in which God has demonstrated His love for you and then praise Him for it.

Consider the above blessings. How many of them do you deserve? How does that knowledge affect your love for God? How will it affect your prayer life?

Plug In:

Father in heaven,

I cannot praise You and thank You enough for Your great mercy and blessings in my life. You are my salvation, my rock and my shield, yet I do not deserve any of that.

As David of old, I marvel that You have taken any thought for me. Thank You for the forgiveness and salvation You have granted me through Jesus Christ.

Thank You for the life and breath You have given me. Thank You for my health and my possessions. Thank You for my family and my friends. Thank You for my brethren.

I will continue to praise You because Your lovingkindness is everlasting.

I love You.

In Your Son's name I pray,

Amen

Praying to the Loving Redeemer

Group Discussion:

What were the most important lessons you learned about prayer this week?

How did this week's readings help your prayer life?

What advice would you give others based on this week's reading to help them pray?

With what issues do you need help or prayers based on this week's reading?

How does God's acceptance of our prayers comfort you?

How has God demonstrated His power in your life?

Why do you think we should pray to God, even though He already knows everything?

What comfort do you gain from knowing God is always with you?

How has God demonstrated love to you?

Plugged In: High Voltage Prayer

WEEK THREE

"Rejoice always, pray without ceasing, in everything give thanks; for this is the will of God in Christ Jesus for you."

I Thessalonians 5:16-18

Plugged In: High Voltage Prayer

Chapter 11

The Humble Prayer

The Good, the Bad and the Arrogant

Do you remember the story of the Pharisee and the tax collector? You can find it in **Luke 18:9-14**.

Also He spoke this parable to some who trusted in themselves that they were righteous, and despised others: "Two men went up to the temple to pray, one a Pharisee and the other a tax collector. The Pharisee stood and prayed thus with himself, 'God, I thank You that I am not like other men-- extortioners, unjust, adulterers, or even as this tax collector. I fast twice a week; I give tithes of all that I possess.'

93

*"And the tax collector, standing afar off, would not so much
as raise his eyes to heaven, but beat his breast, saying, 'God,
be merciful to me a sinner!'*

*"I tell you, this man went down to his house justified rather
than the other; for everyone who exalts himself will be humbled, and he who humbles himself will be exalted."*

"God, I thank You that I am not like other men..." While
the Pharisee paid lip service to thanking God, we cannot help
but notice whom he really praised—not God, but himself. In
fact, while he said, "God, I thank you," it sounds more like he
meant, "God, you should thank me."

Jesus said the Pharisee did not go away justified, but the tax
collector did. What did the tax collector do? He simply recognized how bad he was in the presence of the supremely good
God.

He prayed, "God, be merciful to me a sinner!"

Check the humility. The tax collector would not even raise
his eyes to heaven, but beat his breast in personal distress at his
own sinfulness. By contrasting the Pharisee and the tax collector, we can notice the keys to humility and the keys to humble
prayer.

First, we must not trust in ourselves. Trust in self is what
caused Jesus to tell this parable. He was dealing with people
who "trusted in themselves that they were righteous." We must
not waste our time focusing on the good things we have done.
We must certainly not waste our prayer cataloguing all the
good we have done. The Pharisee did that.

We must remember to whom we are speaking in prayer. Do
we really think we can impress God with our good works?
Isaiah 64:6 says, "All our righteousnesses are like filthy rags."

We will gain no ground with God by listing all our good
works. Our sins rise above our heads. Instead, we must wholly

trust in God's mercy. The tax collector trusted God's mercy and he went away justified.

Second, we must not compare ourselves to others. The Pharisee trusted in his good works because he used the wrong standard of measurement. Anyone can find somebody who has sinned more. But other men are not the standard.

What is the standard? **I Peter 1:15-16** says, "But as He who called you is holy, you also be holy in all your conduct." **Romans 3:23** says, "For all have sinned and fall short of God's glory." Other men are not the standard—God is. We are not holy because we are better than other men. We are not sinners because we are worse than other men. We are holy when we are like God and we are sinners when we fall short of God. I am sure you know where that puts even the best among us.

If we will maintain humility in our lives and our prayers, we must compare ourselves to God. The tax collector compared himself to God and he went away justified.

Third, we must recognize we need God. The Pharisee focused on all he provided for God. But God needs nothing from us and we can provide nothing for Him. **Psalm 50:12** says, "If I were hungry, I would not tell you; for the world is Mine and all its fullness." I am among the first to teach obedience and service in the Lord's kingdom. I admit that without obedience, we will not be saved. **II Thessalonians 1:7-8** says, "…when the Lord Jesus is revealed from heaven with His mighty angels, in flaming fire taking vengeance on those who do not know God, and on those who do not obey the gospel of our Lord Jesus Christ."

While we must obey, we must not believe we are providing God's needs or adding value to God through our obedience. Paul, who clearly taught obedience in the above passage, also said, "God, who made the world and everything in it, since He is Lord of heaven and earth, does not dwell in temples made with hands. Nor is He worshiped with men's hands, as though

He needed anything, since He gives to all life, breath and all things" (**Acts 17:24-25**).

If we will maintain humility in our lives and in our prayers, we must remember that we obey and we pray because we need something from God. We need what the tax collector needed—mercy. The tax collector recognized that he needed something from God and he went away justified.

Finally, we must make sure we are honest with ourselves and God. According to **Matthew 23:14** the Pharisees devoured widows houses while making a pretense of spirituality with long prayer. That is called extortion. According to **Matthew 23:23**, the Pharisees may have tithed well, but they neglected the weightier matters of the law including justice. Despite the rosy self-portrait painted in the Pharisee's prayer, the truth was quite ugly. The Pharisees were in fact extortioners and had neglected justice.

The Pharisee did not look at himself honestly. **Romans 12:3** says, "For I say...to everyone who is among you, not to think of himself more highly than he ought to think." It is hard to be completely honest with ourselves. We tend to look on the bright side of things. We need to turn the critical eye we often have for others on to ourselves. (At the same time, we need to turn the benevolent eye we often have for ourselves toward others.)

We must, however, learn to be completely honest with ourselves and with God. Do not forget what we have already learned. God already knows what we have done, why not go ahead and confess it to Him? Do we really think we can hide the dark side of our lives from Him? The tax collector was completely honest with himself and confessed honestly to God and he went away justified.

Unprofitable Servants

Jesus wanted to drive home our need for humility in **Luke 17:7-10**.

> *And which of you, having a servant plowing or tending sheep, will say to him when he has come in from the field, "Come at once and sit down to eat"? But will he not rather say to him, "Prepare something for my supper, and gird yourself and serve me till I have eaten and drunk, and afterward you will eat and drink"? Does he thank that servant because he did the things that were commanded him? I think not. So likewise you, when you have done all those things which you are commanded, say, "We are unprofitable servants. We have done what was our duty to do."*

We are not familiar with servanthood. As we can imagine, the life of a servant was not one of ease and luxury. It was a life of hard work for the master, even when serving a good master.

Jesus explained that a servant would work all day in the field and when he came inside, he did not get to rest. Instead, he had to serve dinner to his master. What selfless service. What true humility. Surely the master should be grateful and bestow great accolades of praise and thanksgiving on the servant.

But Jesus said, as the disciples knew, that is not how it worked. Why not? Because the servant was simply doing his job. I know this does not set well with modern sensibilities. We tend to believe people deserve great amounts of praise for doing what they should have done anyway. Amazingly enough, when people do what they know is wrong, we often do not blame them but blame those who did not praise them enough for doing their duty. Right or wrong, that is not the way it worked with servants in Jesus' day.

Jesus explained that when we do what God has commanded, no matter how difficult (for instance forgiving a brother seven times in a day—**Luke 17:4**), we are doing only what we should have been doing all along. We have sinned. No amount of doing good today can pay for yesterday's sins. When we live righteously today we are not earning anything, we are only living the way we should have all along.

I remember as a child learning a similar lesson when my dad explained I would never get an allowance for emptying the dishwasher or taking out the trash. As part of the family, those things were simply my duty. Further, there was no sense in expecting my parents to fall all over themselves just because I took the trash out without being reminded. That was my job.

We must recognize the great stumbling block in this arena for us. The sad fact is too many Christians have bought the devil's lie that we deserve what we ask for. All of the complaints from Christians saying, "I prayed, why didn't anything happen?" are arrogance. We must come to God with faith that He can do what we ask and He will do what is best, but never that He ought to do what we ask. We must remove this pride and pray with humility.

I find it ironic that we have a problem with this issue today. We are big on grace. We bask in God's grace and argue about how little we have to do to be saved or receive other blessings from God because of grace. At the same time, however, many of us go to God and ask for His blessing as if we were asking for something other than grace—as if we deserved our requests. Remember grace is a gift; it is, as often defined, unmerited favor. If we have not merited our request, then if God refuses to grant it to us, we have absolutely no room to complain.

We read a great example of humble prayer in **Revelation 4:10-11**:

> *The twenty-four elders fall down before Him who sits on the throne and worship Him who lives forever and ever, and cast their crowns before the throne, saying: "You are worthy, O*

Lord, to receive glory and honor and power; for You created all things, and by Your will they exist and were created."

The 24 royal elders understood they were completely unworthy in the presence of the real King. When they prayed, they removed even the pretense of personal honor and worth and cast their crowns before the only worthy One. That was humility.

One of the great aspects of our God, however, is that while we deserve nothing from Him, He does want to bless us. In the Sermon on the Mount, Jesus taught, "If you then, being evil, know how to give good gifts to your children, how much more will your Father who is in heaven give good things to those who ask Him!" (**Matthew 7:11**).

Humility's Blessings

Our society does not like the idea of humility. In fact, we are practically raised to constantly let everyone know how awesome we are. After all, if we do not tell them, who will?

I remind you of **Romans 12:2**: "Do not be conformed to this world, but be transformed by the renewing of your mind, that you may prove what is that good and acceptable and perfect will of God." We must be different. Perhaps we will not receive the accolades of men, but consider the benefits God's word promises the humble.

We know **I Peter 5:5-6** (plus the numerous repetitions of this in **Proverbs**): "All of you be submissive to one another, and be clothed with humility, for 'God resists the proud, but gives grace to the humble.'"

According to **Psalm 25:9**, "The humble He guides in justice, and the humble He teaches His way."

According to **Psalm 18:27**, "For You will save the humble people, but will bring down haughty looks." **Psalm 149:4**, "For

99

the Lord takes pleasure in His people; He will beautify the humble with salvation."

The great blessing in regard to prayer is seen in **Psalm 9:12**: "He does not forget the cry of the humble." **Psalm 10:17**, "Lord, You have heard the desire of the humble; You will prepare their heart; You will cause Your ear to hear."

If you ever feel God is not listening to you, check your humility. Are you coming to Him as the Pharisee, as though you are something special and deserve something? Or are you coming as the tax collector, knowing you deserve nothing but simply relying on God's mercy?

Prayer Challenge:

List some reasons for which you ought to be humble before God.

Read **Job 38-41**. How does God's power and might compare to ours? Reflect on that great difference throughout today.

Plug In:

Great Father in heaven,

"What is man that You are mindful of him?"

Who am I that You are mindful of me? You are powerful and righteous and I am weak and sinful.

Father, please be merciful to me, a sinner. There is nothing I can offer to repay You, though I devote my life to You.

Thank You for Your Son's sacrifice on my behalf, a sacrifice for which I will never be worthy.

Please strengthen me to do my duty in Your service without thinking I am something special because of it. You Father are worthy of all praise, glory and honor.

I love You.

In Jesus' name,

Amen

Plugged In: High Voltage Prayer

Chapter 12

The Faithful Prayer

The Tough Passage

> *The effective, fervent prayer of a righteous man avails much. Elijah was a man with a nature like ours, and he prayed earnestly that it would not rain; and it did not rain on the land for three years and six months. And he prayed again, and the heaven gave rain, and the earth produced its fruit.*
>
> *--James 5:16-18*

Does this passage teach we will receive anything under the sun for which we might possibly ask as long as we believe enough that God can and will do it? Does it say we will receive any possible request as long as we pray long enough, hard enough, fervently enough and earnestly enough? Yes and no.

While these verses teach us that the prayer of faith will be granted, they do not teach us that we can faithfully pray our every possible dream into reality.

Regrettably, many people misunderstand the real force and faith described in these passages. Elijah prayed for the rain to stop and it did. Then he prayed for it to start again and it did. Some think therefore that if they believe enough, God will control the weather for them through their prayers. Then, with all manner of conviction, they pray that God will stop the rain for their outdoor wedding.

When it rains anyway, they wonder what went wrong. Did they not have enough faith? Did they not pray hard enough or long enough? Did God not keep His end of the prayer covenant? Or does prayer not work? These kinds of feelings cause well-meaning Christians to stop praying completely, especially if the prayers were about issues more serious than a sunny day for an outdoor wedding.

Elijah's faith was not a blind faith that simply thought God would do whatever he asked. Neither should ours be such a faith. The biblical faith is one based on God's word. "So then faith comes by hearing, and hearing by the word of God" (**Romans 10:17**). Praying with faith means praying based upon God's word. That is, we can pray knowing God will do what He has promised. However, we have to believe He will do it.

Consider another passage from **James 1:5-8**:

If any of you lacks wisdom, let him ask of God, who gives to all liberally and without reproach, and it will be given to him. But let him ask in faith, with no doubting, for he who doubts is like a wave of the sea driven and tossed by the wind. For let not that man suppose that he will receive anything from the Lord; he is a double-minded man, unstable in all his ways.

This passage exactly demonstrates the issue of prayer and faith. We can pray the prayer requesting wisdom with faith because God has promised through His word that He will grant that request. He provided two stipulations. One, we must ask. Two, we must ask believing that He will do what He has promised.

After saying all of that, however, we look again at Elijah's prayer and wonder how it fits the above model of faithful prayer? Was it a whimsical wish for rain to cease and start again? No. His was a prayer of faith, believing **Deuteronomy 11:16-17**:

> *Take heed to yourselves, lest your heart be deceived, and you turn aside and serve other gods and worship them, lest the Lord's anger be aroused against you, and He shut up the heavens so that there be no rain, and the land yield no produce, and you perish quickly from the good land which the Lord is giving you.*

God had promised the Israelites He would shut off the rain if they went into idolatry. Israel, under Ahab, was completely idolatrous. In **I Kings 17:1**, Elijah prayed for God to do what He promised; and Elijah believed He would do it. This is the prayer of faith that God will always grant.

Anything You Ask

Another thought provoking pair of passages is **Matthew 21:22** and **Mark 11:24**. These parallel passages both say, "And whatever things you ask in prayer, believing, you will receive." Add the Lord's comment in **John 16:23**, "Most assuredly, I say to you, whatever you ask the Father in My name He will give you."

Combining these three passages, many Christians get the idea that prayer cinches everything. "I prayed about it, it will happen." False teachers of all sorts have exploited these passages to propagate the "name it and claim it" heresy, which reduces prayer to a magic wish to control God.

105

However, we cannot remove these passages from their biblical context. Just as **John 3:16** does not contain everything we need to know about salvation, neither do these passages contain everything we need to know about faithful prayers and their answers. In a later chapter we will look at reasons for which God says, "No." Suffice it to say here, God always reserves the right to refuse our prayers. Consider Jesus' prayer in the Garden for the cup of the crucifixion to pass from Him. Do you think He prayed properly?

One key to note is the modification Jesus made in **John 16:23**. Whatever is asked in His name will be granted. This does not mean any prayer ended with the words "in Jesus' name" will come to pass. Rather, it teaches that when we pray with the authority that comes from Christ, our prayer will be granted.

That takes us right back to Elijah's prayer. When our prayers correspond with the promises of God in His word, they will certainly take place.

Of course, some will say, "That is not fair. What is the good of prayer if it will only be granted when it corresponds with God's will?" This mindset displays a great error in most of the prayers and most of the teaching on prayer today. Regrettably, we spend most of our prayers trying to bend God to our will. Effective prayer, however, is the means by which we bend to God's will. This is the great key to effective prayer. When we mold ourselves to God's will, wanting what He wants and glorifying Him, then our prayers will always be granted and we can pray with faith in Jesus' name.

Faith In God

When we talk about faithful prayer, we must understand exactly in what we are to place our faith. Or, in Whom, I should say.

Too often our faith is in prayer. Some believe if they have prayed enough that settles it, it will come to pass. When it does not, they think prayer does not work. Actually, they are right. Prayer does not work. God does.

Some have faith in faith. That is, they think if they believe enough, their prayers must be granted. When their requests go ungranted, they question their own faith. While we must pray in faith, our faith does not make anything happen. God's power does.

We can pray repeatedly and without ceasing as the persistent widow of **Luke 18** and we may pray with enough faith to move mountains, but the power is Gods and He reserves the right to simply say, "No." Our faith must not be in our faith or in our prayer. It must be in our God. When our faith is in God, we can accept His answers with greater contentment.

A Prayer In Faith

If God reserves the right to say, "No," then praying in faith does not necessarily mean believing He will say, "Yes." Praying in faith means we trust God in four areas. When we pray with these areas of faith, God will always be content with our prayers and we will always be content with God's answers.

First, we must trust that God wants our prayers. Too many get caught in philosophical arguing about prayer and never pray. But God wants us to pray. He commands us to in **I Thessalonians 5:17**: "Pray without ceasing."

Second, we must trust God's ability. He can do all that we ask and what we cannot even imagine asking. As **Ephesians 3:20** says, He "is able to do exceedingly abundantly above all we ask or think."

Third, we must trust God to keep His promises. When our prayers coincide with God's revealed will, we must believe not only that He can but also that He will accomplish them. As **I Corinthians 1:9** says, "God is faithful." He will do what He has promised.

Finally, when we pray for issues about which God has not revealed His will, we must trust His lovingkindness. God loves us and God gives only good gifts. If we ask Him for a fish, He will not give us a snake:

> *Or what man is there among you who, if his son asks for bread, will give him a stone? Or if he asks for a fish, will he give him a serpent. If you then, being evil, know how to give good gifts to your children, how much more will your Father who is in heaven give good things to those who ask Him? (Matthew 7:9-11).*

Regarding this last point, consider Paul's experience in **II Corinthians 12:7-10**:

> *And lest I should be exalted above measure by the abundance of the revelations, a thorn in the flesh was given to me, a messenger of Satan to buffet me, lest I be exalted above measure. Concerning this thing I pleaded with the Lord three times that it might depart from me. And He said to me, "My grace is sufficient for you, for My strength is made perfect in weakness."*

Paul prayed three times for a thorn in the flesh to be removed. If his prayer had been granted, he was more likely to exalt himself with pride. The salvation that came through humility and having to trust God was a greater gift than removing the thorn. Paul unknowingly asked for a snake, but God would only give him a fish. That is God's lovingkindness, even if we do not always recognize it.

Prayer Challenge:

Make a list of your common requests about which God has made no promises. How can you pray in faith for these?

Now, list as many of God's promises you can think of. How can your prayers correspond with those promises?

Plug In:

Father,

I believe. Please help me overcome my doubts and strengthen my faith through Your holy word.

Thank You for Your promises. I am so grateful for Your salvation and ask You to strengthen me to be conformed to the image of Your Son. Please, strengthen Your church here to boldly proclaim Your gospel in wisdom and truth.

Help me submit to Your will in every aspect of my life. Thank You for not submitting to my every whim but providing me with good gifts. Help me always trust Your lovingkindness. You have done so much for me and I do not deserve it. Thank You.

I love You.

In Jesus' name I pray,

Amen

Chapter 13

The Obedient Prayer

Lift Holy Hands

We spend so much time arguing over the propriety of holding hands up during assemblies I am afraid we may have missed the real emphasis of **I Timothy 2:8**: "I desire therefore that the men pray everywhere, lifting up holy hands, without wrath and doubting." Paul's emphasis was not about lifting hands but lifting *holy* hands.

One possible prayer stance is to face the heavens with hands outstretched toward God. But God does not want us to believe we can stretch our hands out to do evil and then turn around and stretch our hands out to Him. If we are going to lift our hands, they must be holy.

Within the context of the verse, Paul provides a contrast. Instead of pointing debating fingers or shaking angry fists at God because we doubt or do not like what He says, we lift holy hands to Him. That is, we lift hands that, having trusted God, have obeyed what He has said.

James 1:19-21 makes a similar point: "So then, my beloved brethren, let every man be swift to hear, slow to speak, slow to wrath; ... receive with meekness the implanted word, which is able to save your souls." In our dealing with God, we must be quick to hear, but slow to speak and slow to anger.

While we often apply **James 1:19** to our relationships with men, James applied it to our relationship with God's word. Instead of speaking against or being angry with His word, we need to hear and obey His word.

At the same time, this picture of holy hands is not just about our actions toward God, but also our relationships with others. We must not believe we can lift our hands to God at night, if we have been lifting our hands in violence, anger or dissension against others throughout the day. God wants holy hands.

The Disobedient Prayer

Examine **Isaiah 59:1-8**:

Behold, the LORD'S hand is not shortened, That it cannot save; Nor His ear heavy, That it cannot hear. But your iniquities have separated you from your God; And your sins have hidden His face from you, So that He will not hear. For your hands are defiled with blood, And your fingers with iniquity; Your lips have spoken lies, Your tongue has muttered perversity. No one calls for justice, Nor does any plead for truth. They trust in empty words and speak lies; They conceive evil and bring forth iniquity. They hatch vipers' eggs and weave the spider's web; He who eats of their eggs dies, And from that which is crushed a viper breaks out. Their

*webs will not become garments, Nor will they cover them-
selves with their works; Their works are works of iniquity,
And the act of violence is in their hands. Their feet run to
evil, And they make haste to shed innocent blood; Their
thoughts are thoughts of iniquity; Wasting and destruction
are in their paths. The way of peace they have not known,
And there is no justice in their ways; They have made themselves crooked paths; Whoever takes that way shall not know
peace.*

Our sins separate us from God such that He will not heed
our prayers. Notice how many times God rebuked the Israelites
for having violent and defiled hands. God will not accept the
prayer of the disobedient, He wants holy hands. We must not
believe we can live in all manner of sin and then have access to
God's throne in prayer.

The Pharisees needed to learn this principle. In **Matthew
23:14**, they offered long prayers to show how spiritual they
were. But behind the scenes they devoured widows' houses.
Perhaps that is why, when He described the Pharisee's prayer
in **Luke 18:11**, Jesus said he "prayed thus with himself." His
prayer was not getting to God.

Read **Isaiah 66:3-4**:

*He who kills a bull is as if he slays a man; he who sacrifices
a lamb, as if he breaks a dog's neck; he who offers a grain
offering, as if he offers swine's blood; he who burns incense,
as if he blesses an idol. Just as they have chosen their own
ways, and their soul delights in their abominations, so will I
choose their delusions, and bring their fears on them; because when I called, no one answered, when I spoke they did
not hear; but they did evil before My eyes, and chose that in
which I do not delight.*

What a power-packed passage. If we will not hear when
God speaks to us, how can we expect God to hear when we
speak to Him?

In this passage, Israelites were rebelling against God's word, but they were offering sacrifices. Surely these acts of worship and sacrifice, which were to be for the forgiveness of sins, made up for all the sins they committed. But God said they might as well have killed a man as to sacrifice a bull in their rebellious state.

If we live in disobedience, God views our prayers the same way. We might as well curse God as seek His blessing if we are living in rebellion. We can only pray effectively, when our prayers naturally flow from an obedient life.

Whom God Hears

"The eyes of the Lord are on the righteous, and His ears are open to their cry," David said in **Psalm 34:15**. He had just described the life of righteousness saying, "Keep your tongue from evil, and your lips from speaking deceit. Depart from evil and do good; seek peace and pursue it" (**Psalm 34:13-14**).

In **I Peter 3:10-12**, Peter used this passage to support his plea for good relationships. He said we should be compassionate, tender-hearted, courteous, loving, not returning evil for evil or reviling for reviling but rather give a blessing. This person God hears.

Intriguingly, Peter had just given a very specific example about righteousness and prayers. In **I Peter 3:7**, he explained that husbands must live righteously with their wives, otherwise their prayers will be hindered.

The long and short of this is we must be obedient prayers. Otherwise, as we have all heard, our prayers get no higher than the rafters.

But I Have Already Messed This Up

At this point, a certain dread may be settling on your shoulders. If we have to be obedient to be heard in prayer, we have already botched it, haven't we? We have all already disobeyed. "For all have sinned and fall short of the glory of God" (**Romans 3:23**). What can we do?

Read **Isaiah 66:2**, just before God said how He would deal with the prayers of the rebellious, He explained how He would deal with the prayers of the penitent. "But on this one will I look: On Him who is poor and of a contrite spirit, and who trembles at My word."

God hears and heeds the prayers of penitent saints. Consider David's example in **Psalm 32**. For a time, David was silent about his sin (perhaps referring to his sin with Bathsheba and Uriah). During that time, God's hand of discipline was heavy. However, when he finally contritely admitted his sin to the Lord, God heard and David was forgiven.

Would you like to see an example of the contrite heart? Read **Psalm 38**. Read the words of a man whose heart is broken over his sins. The psalm is too lengthy to include here. Yet it tells of a man who desperately wanted God's help. He knew he had let God down. He recognized he had no right to expect God to hear his words, because at some time he had refused to heed God's word. Yet he prayed all the same.

What a powerful statement he made in **vs. 15**. "For in You, O Lord, I hope: You will hear, O Lord my God." David, without conceit or arrogance, knew he could trust God to hear his prayer. Not because he, David, deserved to be heard. But rather, because he knew God's promise to mercifully hear the brokenhearted.

When our hearts are broken over our sins, God will hear our confession and our pleas. The question is, are we really this brokenhearted over our sins?

Prayer Challenge:

Examine your life. **Psalm 66:18** says, "If I regard iniquity in my heart, the Lord will not hear." That is, if we are ignoring our own sins and holding on to some of them in our hearts, God will not listen to our prayers. Are there any sins you have been regarding in your heart? If so, break your heart and repent now.

Read **Psalm 38**. Have you been this broken hearted over your sins? How would this kind of contrition be manifested in our daily lives?

Plug In:

All wise heavenly Father,

My sins are too numerous to count. Please do not rebuke me in Your wrath and chasten me in Your burning anger.

I am sorry I have disappointed You in so many ways. My heart throbs within me and You have heard my sighing and groaning, for my iniquities have gone over my head.

Please forgive me, Father. My hope is in You and I know You will answer for You are my salvation.

Father, strengthen me to live by Your holy word. Help me to seek after Your righteousness and Your kingdom. Help me to be conformed to the image of Your precious Son.

To Your word and will I devote myself. I want to present holy hands to You, for You are holy.

Thank You for Your forgiveness.

I love You.

In the Savior's name I pray,

Amen

Plugged In: High Voltage Prayer

Chapter 14

The Dependent Prayer

The Lonely God?

I know his heart was in the right place. He was trying to get people to pray more. However, whoever first portrayed Jehovah as the lonely God missed the boat. God did not create us because He was lonely. He did not ask us to pray because His emotional well-being depends on having puny humans talk to Him.

This concept does nothing less than remake God in our image. We become lonely and want companionship and conversation. We may, therefore, think that is why God made us and wants us to pray. Absolutely not!

God rebuked the wicked of Israel in **Psalm 50:21** saying, "You thought that I was altogether like you; but I will rebuke you."

In that same psalm, God talked about the Old Testament sacrifices. Why did He ask for those? Not because He needed them. He explained in **vs. 12**, "If I were hungry, I would not tell you; for the world is Mine, and all its fullness."

It seems some of the Israelites were living sinfully but thought their relationship with God was fine because they were serving God, feeding Him with their sacrifices. However, God did not need to be fed. God did not ask for sacrifices because He needed food; He asked for sacrifices because the Israelites needed the deliverance He would grant them through their sacrifices. "Call upon Me in the day of trouble; I will deliver you, and you shall glorify Me" (**vs. 15**).

In the same vein, God has not asked for our prayers because He needs companionship. Rather, we need God's grace. Therefore, we must pray.

Thinking Too Highly

Paul warned us not to think too highly of ourselves in **Romans 12:3**. Rather, we need to be sober-minded and realize we are where we are because of God's grace.

How easily we can think too much of ourselves. How easily we can think we have provided for ourselves. After all, we did the work that earned the money that put the food on the tables, the roof over our heads and the clothes on our backs. How easy it is to think we are independent of God.

However, that is not the case. We do depend on God. We must pray dependently like Jabez in **I Chronicles 4:9-10**. "And Jabez called on the God of Israel, saying, 'Oh, that You would bless me indeed, and enlarge my territory, that Your hand would be with me, and that You would keep me from evil, that I may not cause pain.' So God granted him what he requested."

One of the problems with the modern hooplah surrounding Jabez' prayer is it misses the forest for the trees. We must not get so caught up in the specific requests in Jabez' prayer, that we miss the most important point. Jabez prayed.

Why did Jabez pray? Because He knew from Whom all blessings flow. How would he be blessed? How would his territory be enlarged? How would he be kept from evil? Only by God's good hand.

Jabez was more honorable than his brothers, because Jabez prayed dependently.

Work And Pray

Perhaps you have heard the great saying, "Pray like it all depends on God. But work like it all depends on you." This contains the crux of dependent praying.

Ephesians 3:20 provides a basis for this adage. "Now to Him who is able to do exceedingly abundantly above all that we ask or think, according to the power that works in us..."

We need to depend on God in prayer because He can do more than we ask or think. However, He does so by the power working in us. God often works through us to provide the answers to our prayers. That is why it often looks like we are doing the work.

For most of us, God answers our prayers for food, shelter and clothing by giving us the ability to work, manage money and buy what we need. He answers our prayer for wisdom by giving us the ability to read and study His word, seek good counselors and learn from our experience. He answers our prayers for good relationships by teaching us how to behave properly.

We must always recognize that while God may use us in the answers to our prayers, if He backed out, we would be lost.

That Depends On God

What does God control that we need? Examine these passages and see.

The farmer who thinks he works hard sowing and reaping and is independent of God should remember that God sends forth the rain and the sunshine—**Matthew 5:45**. From where would our food come if God stopped that?

The worker who believes he has paid for all his goods by the sweat of his own brow and is independent of God should remember that it is by God that we live, move and have our very being—**Acts 17:28**. What could we accomplish if God stopped that?

The wealthy man who believes he has bought all things for himself by his own financial savvy needs to remember that every good gift comes from the Father of lights—**James 1:17**. Where would he be if God stopped that?

Of course, let us not forget the most important of all God's blessings. Left to ourselves, we are all on a one-way path to hell. But by God's grace we can be His adopted heirs, redeemed by His Son's blood and awaiting a heavenly inheritance—**Ephesians 1:3-14**. Where would we be if God stopped that?

Looking at it this way, we understand the admonition in **Proverbs 3:6**, "In all your ways acknowledge Him." Everything we have and are has come from God; we need to acknowledge His hand in our lives.

Only with this understanding of our dependence can we pray the dependent prayer.

Prayer Challenge:

"In all your ways acknowledge Him" (**Proverbs 3:6**). List how the hand of God has been involved in your life and blessings.

How would your prayer life be different if you prayed like everything depended on God? Pray like that today.

Plug In:

Father in heaven,

You have done so much for me and I can do so little for You.

I know You do not need anything I have to offer. However, I am thankful that You accept what I offer anyway.

Thank You, Father, for the abilities You have granted me. Thank You for the work You have allowed me to do. Thank You for the material blessings You have granted me through that work. Thank You for my family, my brethren and my friends whom You use to strengthen me.

Thank You for the grace You have bestowed through Your Son's sacrifice and through Your Spirit's revelation. Help me to live by Your word.

Thank You for allowing me to pray to You.

Father, I know You do not need me, but I need You. Thank You for being my Father.

I love You.

In Your Son's name I pray,

Amen

Chapter 15

The Fearful Prayer

Keeping The Balance

In ***The God of the Towel***, Jim McGuiggan wrote, "It seems we're ever in need of balance. We're either jauntily talking about what we will or will not say when we meet the holy God, or we're afraid to even hint that we'll be graciously received by him for the sake of Christ our Savior. Some of us assume a breezy familiarity with 'our good friend, God,' while others have never come to trust the love of God toward them in Jesus Christ" (p. 95).

While I am told by many that they grew up in a time when the balance was tipped to the hellfire and brimstone, fear side of serving God, we must be careful not to swing the balance too far the other way.

We live in a day and age when men tell us we can speak to God the same way we do our best friend and we can call Him "daddy" in our prayers because that is supposedly what "Abba" meant.

I struggle with that. While, I question that supposed interpretation of "Abba," I am well aware God is our friend and our tender Father. Yet He still remains the august and powerful sovereign ruler of the universe. He is the holy power behind the universe. We cannot saunter into His presence, snap our fingers under His nose and brazenly wisecrack our way through our conversations with Him. He is God, we must fear and respect Him. We must be awed when we come into His presence. Even Jesus, God the Son, prayed with fear. **Hebrews 5:7** says, "Who, in the days of His flesh, when He had offered up prayers and supplications, with vehement cries and tears to Him who was able to save Him from death, and was heard because of His godly fear."

No doubt, as McGuiggan rightly stated, "We're ever in need of balance."

Goodness And Severity

Paul addressed balance in **Romans 11:22**. He said, "Consider the goodness and severity of God: on those who fell, severity; but toward you, goodness, if you continue in His goodness. Otherwise you also will be cut off."

Paul feared some of the Gentile Christians might become self-satisfied with the grace they had received. He was especially concerned with this when they understood that Jews had been cut off from God.

Paul reminded them that God, who had cut off natural branches from His tree, could cut off the grafted branches as well: "For if God did not spare the natural branches, He may not spare you either" (**Romans 11:21**). That is, if God could cut off Jews, He could also cut off Gentiles.

Therefore we must not strut into the presence of God acting as though we deserve what we are being given. We need to enter God's presence with the fear and humility that accompanies the person who knows the punishment he or she really deserves.

How Would You Live?

Think about this—how would you act if you had been forgiven by a king, or even just a friend, for a great betrayal?

Would you not live as best you could not to upset that person again? You would be afraid he or she might drudge up the past and bring the punishment upon you—a punishment that you deserve.

Why would we deal any differently with God? Because God is so gracious, we sometimes act as though we can treat Him in ways we would treat no one else.

Our fear of God should not only affect how we pray, but our entire lives. Remember the parable of the unforgiving servant in **Matthew 18**. He had been forgiven a great debt. Instead of fearing his deserved punishment would be given to him anyway, he simply used his king's grace as a means to sin. He refused to offer the same forgiveness to another.

When his king heard about it, he had the man arrested and thrown into prison. He brought the initial deserved punishment upon him.

We are that servant who has been granted forgiveness of a great debt. We must not use that grace as a license for further sin. As Paul said in **Romans 6:1-2**, "What shall we say then? Shall we continue in sin that grace may abound? Certainly not. How shall we who died to sin live any longer in it?"

Even as Christians we must fear God and the punishment He will bring on those who turn from Him. That fear will cause us to continue steadfastly in His word. Continuing steadfastly in His word will cause us to be pleasing to God, giving Him no cause to call us back into His presence to strip His forgiveness away from us.

Love And Fear Him

Regrettably, this is all clouded by our modern debate regarding whether we should be moved more by love or fear. God, however, does not view love and fear as we do. We think emotionally about love and fear; therefore, we see them as opposites. Because God thinks of them behaviorally, He sees love and fear as practically interchangeable.

Read **Deuteronomy 10-13** and see the comparisons.

Deuteronomy 10:12 says fearing God means walking in God's ways. In **11:22**, loving God means that.

In **Deuteronomy 11:1** loving God means keeping His commandments. However in **13:4** keeping His commandments means you fear Him.

In **Deuteronomy 10:20** serving God means you fear Him. Yet in **10:12** service means love.

In **Deuteronomy 11:22** loving God means you will hold fast to Him. However in **10:20** if you hold fast to God, it means you fear Him.

Finally, while we may view love and fear as opposites, the Bible never presents them as such. In fact, love and fear have the same opposite—hatred.

In **Matthew 6:24** love and hate are presented as opposites: "No one can serve two masters; for either he will hate the one and love the other…"

Fear and hate are also presented as opposites in **Proverbs 13:13**: "He who despises the word will be destroyed, but he who fears the commandment will be rewarded."

Love and fear are almost interchangeable, but not quite. Both are about obedience and service. However, love is obediently serving God because of what He has already done for us. As **I John 4:19** says, "We love Him because He first loved us."

Fear, on the other hand, is obediently serving God because of what He can do to us. **Matthew 10:28** teaches us this. We must not fear men; all they can do is kill the body. But God can kill the body and afterward cast the soul and body into hell. Therefore we must fear Him.

Do not spend your time fretting whether you have your love versus fear out of whack. Simply obey God and you will both love and fear Him.

The conclusion of the whole matter is that we must not get uppity in our prayer lives. We can take comfort, knowing that God allows us to pray to Him. In that sense, we can come boldly into His presence through Jesus' blood (**Hebrews 10:19**). However, we do not deserve to pray. We must not come into God's presence as though we do. We must maintain the humility, the awe, the fear that accompanies God's presence.

Prayer Challenge:

What has God done for you, causing you to love Him?

What do you deserve from God, causing you to fear Him?

How do your prayer life and your life in general need to change to reflect a healthy fear of God?

Plug In:

Almighty God in Heaven,

You are more powerful than I can imagine. I am more sinful than I can fathom.

Thank You for letting me come confidently into Your presence, praying to You despite my sinfulness.

Father, I thank You for Your grace that washes my sins away through Your Son's blood. I ask for Your continued mercy. Please be merciful to me a sinner.

Help me stand in awe of You. I am sorry if I have ever treated our relationship flippantly. I am sorry if I have not revered and feared You as You deserve. Please forgive me.

Help me be like Your Son. Help me obey and fear You with godly fear.

I love You.

In Jesus' name I pray,

Amen

Group Discussion:

What were the most important lessons you learned about prayer this week?

How did this week's readings help your prayer life?

What advice would you give others based on this week's reading to help them pray?

With what issues do you need help or prayers based on this week's reading?

How can we demonstrate humility in our prayers?

What does it mean to pray in faith?

Why is an obedient life and important part of having a positive prayer life?

For what are we dependent on God (be specific)?

How can we maintain a healthy fear of God and how does that impact our prayers?

WEEK FOUR

"Make a joyful shout to the Lord, all you lands! Serve the Lord with gladness; Come before His presence with singing. Know that the Lord, he is God; It is He who has made us and not we ourselves; We are His people and the sheep of His pasture. Enter into His gates with thanksgiving, and into His courts with praise. Be thankful to Him, and bless His name. For the Lord is good; His mercy is everlasting, and His truth endures to all generations."

Psalm 100

Chapter 16

The Unselfish Prayer

A Proper Perspective

What is the most often recognized aspect of prayer? Petition.

That being the case, we can easily lose the proper perspective on prayer. If we are not careful, prayer may become a selfish and self-centered exercise, reciting our own personal wish list. Nothing about our Christianity is allowed to be selfish or self-centered; prayer is no exception.

Paul told the Philippians, "Let nothing be done through selfish ambition or conceit, but in lowliness of mind let each esteem others better than himself. Let each of you look out not only for his own interests, but also for the interests of others" (**Philippians 2:3-4**).

James 3:14-16 makes an even stronger plea against self-ishness: "If you have bitter envy and self-seeking in your hearts, do not boast and lie against the truth. This wisdom does not descend from above, but is earthly, sensual, demonic. For where envy and self-seeking exist, confusion and every evil thing are there."

Whoa! That is pretty powerful stuff. That is pretty frightening stuff. Did he say when we are being selfish we are being earthly, sensual and *demonic*? He sure did.

James says we should be pure, peaceable, gentle, willing to yield, full of mercy and good fruits, without partiality and without hypocrisy instead of being wrapped up in our own self-ishness (**James 3:17-18**). When these attributes govern our lives, they will also govern our prayers.

Do Not Ask Amiss

James also hit directly on selfish, self-seeking requests. While God certainly has granted us the privilege to ask Him for anything we want, He provided some guidelines for our petitions. In **James 4:2-3**, he wrote, "You do not have because you do not ask. You ask and do not receive, because you ask amiss, that you may spend it on your pleasures."

When we are making requests, what are they about? Why do we want that new house, that new car or that new job? Are we simply thinking about ourselves and our own personal pleasures?

Here is a tough one—why do we want to recover from that illness? Is it simply because of all we might miss out on if we died right now? Or why do we want that loved one to recover from her illness? Is it simply because of all we would lose if she were gone?

These are tough questions. We are allowed to ask for things we want. Paul wanted the thorn in the flesh removed and he was allowed to pray for it (**II Corinthians 12:8**). Hezekiah wanted to live longer and he was allowed to pray for it (**II Kings 20:3**). However, we must check our motivation. If we are simply asking for things to spend on our own selfish pleasures, we must not expect God to grant our requests.

Do not misunderstand. I have no doubt that at times God is willing to grant requests simply as a benevolent gift to His children when they ask. I am sure He does so at times, simply because they ask Him.

However, there are two issues we need to understand. First, if we are simply asking for a gift to spend on our own pleasure, we cannot expect God to give it to us. Second, if He does bestow the blessing, be sure that He expects His gifts to be used to serve Him and others.

I Peter 4:10-11 says:

As each one has received a gift, minister it to one another, as good stewards of the manifold grace of God. If anyone speaks, let him speak as the oracles of God. If anyone ministers, let him do it as with the ability which God supplies, that in all things God may be glorified through Jesus Christ, to whom belong the glory and the dominion forever and ever. Amen.

Praying Properly

When we pray, instead of focusing on ourselves, we should give thought to God and to others. Praying unselfishly recognizes that while prayer includes requests, it is not simply a wish list. God is not some cosmic Santa Clause; we must not pray as though He is.

Praying unselfishly means that while we should lay our cares and concerns out before the Lord because He cares for us (**I Peter 5:7**), prayer is not merely a laundry list of complaints.

Praying unselfishly means praying in submission to God's will. We will discuss this more in a later chapter, but for now, suffice it to say we need to follow Jesus' example in the garden. He was certainly allowed to pray that the cup be passed from Him. However, He was not selfish in His prayer. He wanted God's will done over His own.

Further, praying unselfishly means thinking about others. Following the advice of **Philippians 2:3-4**, our prayers should seek others' interests above our own. After all, we are to view others as more important. Therefore, their interests and desires are more important and it is more important to pray for their interests and desires.

When we come to God in prayer we should follow Paul's words in **Romans 12:15**, rejoicing with those who rejoice and weeping with those who weep. When others have cause to praise and thank God, we should praise and thank God with them. When others have anxieties and needs to cast before God, we should be right there with them.

Let's let the rubber hit the road here. It is not enough to tell brethren how much we are praying for them, we actually have to do it. That is unselfish prayer.

Praying For Enemies

Perhaps the most unselfish prayer is the blessing on our enemies. The one who prays selfishly would rejoice when his enemy is weeping and weep when his enemy is rejoicing—we must not. The one who prays selfishly would curse when his enemy curses him—we must not.

As the children's song says, "You can talk about me all that you please, I'll talk about you down on my knees."

Jesus said, "Bless those who curse you, do good to those who hate you, and pray for those who spitefully use you" (**Matthew 5:44-45**).

Peter told the Asian Christians in **I Peter 3:9**, "Not returning evil for evil or reviling for reviling, but on the contrary blessing, knowing that you were called to this, that you may inherit a blessing."

A great example of this unselfish prayer comes from David in **Psalm 35:11-14**:

Fierce witnesses rise up; they ask me things that I do not know. They reward me evil for good, to the sorrow of my soul. But as for me, when they were sick, my clothing was sackcloth; I humbled myself with fasting; and my prayer would return to my own heart. I paced about as though he were my friend or brother; I bowed down heavily, as one who mourns for his mother.

That is unselfish prayer. Could we pray that prayer?

Prayer Challenge:

List any people you consider to be enemies in your life. Pray for them right now.

Think about your friends, family, co-workers (and even your enemies again). For what specific issues in their lives should you spend some time weeping or rejoicing in prayer for them? Don't just list generalities that everyone needs. Think about specific issues in their lives. Then pray for them.

Plug In:

Dear Father,

I praise Your high and holy name. You are above all others and there is none like You.

I pray that Your kingdom and righteousness will be spread over the face of the earth. Please use me to help accomplish Your glory.

I thank You for the food You have granted me to eat, the clothes You have allowed me to wear and the home in which You have allowed me to live. Please continue to bless me that I may be a blessing to others.

Father, please strengthen my brethren that they may with boldness serve You. Be with each of them in their special needs at this time. Help me strengthen and comfort them as well. Strengthen me to rejoice with those who rejoice and weep with those who weep.

I love you, Father.

In Jesus' name I pray,

Amen

Chapter 17

The Thankful Prayer

Enter His Gates

Make a joyful shout to the Lord, all you lands!
Serve the Lord with gladness;
Come before His presence with singing.
Know that the Lord, He is God;
It is He who has made us, and not we ourselves;
We are His people and the sheep of His pasture.

Enter into His gates with thanksgiving,
And into His courts with praise.
Be thankful to Him, and bless His name.

For the Lord is good;
His mercy is everlasting,
And His truth endures to all generations.
Psalm 100

While this psalm originally pictured Old Testament Israel coming to the gates of the temple, it also depicts us as we come into God's presence, entering the holy place by Christ's blood. If Israel was to enter God's gates with thanksgiving, how much more ought we?

When we think of major sins, of what do we think? Murder? Adultery? Homosexuality? Can you imagine ingratitude on that list? Guess what! In **Romans 1:21**, God gave the Gentiles up to uncleanness "because, although they knew God, they did not glorify Him as God, nor were thankful."

In **II Timothy 3:2**, Paul listed being unthankful as one of the sins men will commit in the perilous times when they become lovers of themselves, lovers of money, proud, boastful, slanderers, traitors, etc.

What a shock. When we enter the gates of the Lord it had better be with thanksgiving. As Paul said, "In everything give thanks" (**I Thessalonians 5:18**). Surely, when we consider exactly what God has done for us, being thankful ought to be natural. That is not always the case however.

Where Were The Nine?

It certainly would seem to be natural to thank God, but do you remember the 10 lepers Jesus healed in **Luke 17:11-19**?

In the end, only one thanked Jesus. Our Savior was left asking, "Were there not ten cleansed? But where are the nine?"

I think I can answer the Lord's question.

The first said, "He knows I am thankful, I don't have to say it."

The second said, "I was getting better anyway."

The third said, "I was the one who went to see the priest, Jesus did not do anything."

The fourth said, "I don't see many others giving thanks."

The fifth said, "That Samaritan gave thanks for the rest of us."

The sixth said, "Since it is gone, I must have never had leprosy to begin with."

The seventh said, "The priest must have healed me."

The eighth said, "I'm not sure this will last, I better wait before I give thanks."

The ninth said, "I'll thank Jesus later."

Ok, ok, I made that up. However, does that not sound like many Christians today?

As the song says, we should "Give thanks with a grateful heart." But keep in mind we are actually supposed to give thanks. Being thankful is more than just an attitude of gratitude. It means actually verbalizing our thanks to God. "Let us continually offer the sacrifice of praise to God, that is, the fruit of our lips, giving thanks to His name" (**Hebrews 13:15**).

Remember God's Gifts

Two old friends bumped into one another on the street one day. One looked forlorn, on the verge of tears.

His friend asked, "What has the world done to you, my old friend?"

The sad fellow said, "Let me tell you. Three weeks ago, an uncle died and left me $40,000."

"That's a lot of money."

"But you see, two weeks ago, a cousin I never knew died and left me $85,000."

"Sounds like you have been blessed…"

"But you don't understand!" the sad man interrupted. "Last week my great-aunt died and left me nearly a quarter of a million."

The extremely confused friend asked, "With all of this blessing why do you look so glum?"

"This week…nothing!"

That is the trouble with receiving something on such a regular basis—eventually we come to expect it. If we receive something over a long time, we begin to view it as an entitlement, not a gift.

This can sorely affect our prayer lives. Too often we spend so much time asking for some new blessing tomorrow or complaining because we did not get some blessing yesterday, we forget to thank God for all the blessings we have received up through today.

We do not deserve the comfortable homes in which we live, the great food we eat, the clean water we drink, the nice air we breathe, the good health we enjoy. Yet after enjoying these things for so long, we begin to expect them. We take them for granted. If they are removed for even a short time (for instance, the power lines go down in a storm) we do not learn to be grateful for the times we did have these blessings, we just get upset and complain. We must not take God's lovingkindness in any of its forms for granted, but must always give thanks.

"Oh, that men would give thanks to the Lord for His goodness, and for His wonderful works to the children of men" (**Psalm 107:15**). Consider offering some prayers that are purely prayers of thanksgiving. That is, offer a prayer that confesses no sin and extends no requests. Simply give thanks for everything you can think of. Let me assure you, such a prayer takes discipline and practice. When you try it for the first time, you will be amazed at how easily you naturally slip into petition prayer.

While we are being thankful, we might just begin by thanking God for inviting us to pray. As we have noted throughout our study, we do not deserve that either. Prayer is a gift for which we should be grateful. More than being grateful, we should give thanks for it.

Prayer Challenge:

Make a good list of things for which you should be thankful. List even some of the obvious little things that we can easily take for granted. Pray a prayer that is nothing but thanksgiving.

If you were really governed by thanksgiving all the time, how would that affect the way you live and pray on a daily basis?

Plug In:

Merciful God,

Thank You for allowing me to come into Your presence in prayer. Thank You for allowing me to be Your child and call You Father.

You have blessed me in more ways than I can count. You have granted me life and health. You have given me friends and family. You have brought me into a local congregation. You have taken me into Christ's body. Thank You.

You have blessed me again today, providing my daily needs. I have eaten today. I am clothed today. I have a place to live today. Thank You.

Most of all, thank You for Your grace and mercy. Your Son died for my sins. Your Spirit revealed Your will. You have allowed me to study and understand Your word. Thank You.

Father, may I never take Your gifts for granted. May I acknowledge You in all my ways and always give You thanks.

I love You.

In Jesus' name I pray,

Amen

Chapter 18

The Persistent Prayer

Persistent Praying

We are just past the halfway point in our study of prayer. Perhaps you were already well-established in prayer before this study and this is just helping you in your habit. Perhaps you are using this book as a means to develop a new habit.

If yours is the second case, then perhaps you have already hit that wall that comes with developing a new habit. You have been doing it a while now; missing a day won't hurt, you might think. However, if you miss one day, the second day becomes easier to miss and then the third.

This is a good time to remember that we are to pray persistently. As Paul said in **I Thessalonians 5:17**, "Pray without ceasing." Prayer must be a habit.

David said in **Psalm 55:16-17**, "As for me, I will call upon God, and the Lord shall save me. Evening and morning and at noon I will pray, and cry aloud, and He shall hear my voice."

Praying persistently means praying regularly and habitually. It also means to pray despite circumstances that might hinder prayer.

Consider the example of Daniel in **Daniel 6:10**:

Now when Daniel knew that the writing was signed, he went home. And in his upper room, with his windows open toward Jerusalem, he knelt down on his knees three times that day, and prayed and gave thanks before his God, as was his custom since early days.

Both aspects of persistence are demonstrated in this verse. First, Daniel had the daily habit of three prayer times. He was persistent and habitual in his prayers. Second, the law had just been passed making prayer to Jehovah illegal. Talk about a roadblock. Yet Daniel persisted in prayer anyway.

Consider one other aspect of Daniel's persistent prayer. His co-workers knew he prayed persistently. Further, they were convinced he would persist in prayer even if they outlawed it. What an amazing example. Does anybody know that about us?

As Daniel did, we must pray persistently, no matter who or what opposes us.

Persistent Petitions

While we pray persistently in general, we must also address the issue of persistent requests.

Perhaps you prayed for resolution to some problem today and it did not happen. Perhaps you prayed for a particular blessing today and it did not come. What do you do next?

Keep praying about it. Be persistent.

In **Luke 11:5-8**, Jesus told of a neighbor who persistently knocked on his friend's door asking for help in the middle of the night. Jesus said the friend would eventually grant the request because of the neighbor's persistence. How much more will God, who loves us, grant our prayers if we persist? This is called importuning God.

This prayer is a lot like the little kid who persistently badgers his mother, "Can I have a cookie?" "Can I have a cookie?" "Please, Mom, I really want a cookie." "Johnny has a cookie." "Can I have a cookie?" Many times, the mother, because of the child's persistence, grants the cookie.

The Bible is full of persistent prayers.

In **Luke 6:12** Jesus spent all night in prayer. In **Acts 9:9, 11** Saul prayed for three days without eating and drinking after his vision on the road to Damascus. In **Acts 12:5** the whole church in Jerusalem were constantly praying for Peter.

Nehemiah prayed for days about the broken wall of Jerusalem (**Nehemiah 1:4**). Moses prayed for Israel's salvation from God's wrath for forty days (**Deuteronomy 9:18**).

Should we persist in our requests? Absolutely. Some things are just that important to us. In fact, at times, the Bible picture of persistent prayer seems to be, "God, please grant this."

"Well, I don't know," He replies, "how badly do you want it?"

Has your prayer not been granted? Pray again. Be persistent. The question is, are there any issues we believe are important enough with which to importune God?

No Persistence Guarantee

Please do not misunderstand. While God has said we should be persistent in our requests, He has never promised all persistent petitions will be granted.

We will discuss in a later section why God says, "No," to our prayers at times. Suffice it to say here that God continues to reserve the right to deny any and every request no matter how we persist in it.

We understand this for two very important reasons.

First, we must not believe God will grant our request just because we repeat it ad infinitum. Jesus explained that we must not pray with vain repetitions in **Matthew 6:7**. The repetition becomes vain, as Jesus explained, when we think God must hear us because we are talking so much.

Second, we must understand this lest we pray and pray and pray and do not receive and think there is something wrong with us or with prayer. True, there might be something wrong with us, but not necessarily.

Jesus prayed three times for the cup of suffering to be removed (**Matthew 26:39, 42, 44**). Yet He still endured the suffering of the cross and the burden of our sins, separating Him from the Father.

Paul prayed three times for his thorn in the flesh to be removed (**II Corinthians 12:8**), yet God said, "No."

Neither of these were failed saints. Nor can we say they just did not pray enough. God simply reserves the right to refuse our requests. He is God; that is His right.

How should we deal with that? We must submit to God's will. As Jesus prayed in the garden, "Nevertheless, not as I will, but as You will" (**Matthew 26:39**).

If God grants our request, we should gratefully submit to Him. If He does not, we should still gratefully submit to Him. God has his reasons for denying our requests and we must trust Him and His will.

Further, since we cannot know the mind of God except where He has revealed it to us through His Word, in most cases we cannot know He has finally and ultimately denied our request. We can only know He has not granted our request yet. Therefore, persist in your petition not until you think, "Well, I guess God just isn't going to do this," but until you absolutely know God has denied your request.

David's example in **II Samuel 12:15-23** demonstrates this. Following David's sin with Bathsheba, God said the child must die. David prayed for his child, fervently hoping God would change His mind regarding the judgment. When the child died, David knew his request had finally been denied. At that point, he ceased his fasting and praying for the child and returned to his normal devotion to God.

What an example of persistent prayer while submitting to God. May we also pray both persistently and submissively.

Prayer Challenge:

Renew your commitment to prayer and to this study. Go back to your responses to the Prayer Challenge of Chapter 1 on page 13. Review your commitment made there. If you have been slipping, reinstate your commitment right now. If you haven't been slipping, simply remind yourself of your commitment and keep persisting in prayer.

List any improvements you need to make to your prayer persistence.

Consider your prayer life. Are there any prayers in which you have not persisted that you need to renew? On the other hand, are there any prayers you have allowed to become merely vain repetitions? List them below and correct the situation in your prayers today.

Plug In:

Almighty God,

Your might and power are beyond comprehension. Your grace is beyond understanding. I thank You for Your mercy and blessing.

Father, all too often I fall short in my commitment to prayer. Help me to maintain my devotion to You.

Thank You for allowing me to come to You repeatedly and lay my requests before You. At the same time, please forgive me for the times when my prayers have become vainly repetitive.

Please strengthen me today to serve You faithfully.

I love You.

In Your Son's name,

Amen

Chapter 19

Jesus: The Mediator Of Our Prayers

A Misunderstood Mediator

I believe I have misunderstood what Paul meant in **I Timothy 2:5** for most of my life. "For there is one God and one Mediator between God and men, the Man Christ Jesus." For a long time, this verse presented the following picture to me. While I always addressed my prayers to "my heavenly Father," I envisioned the prayer actually going to Jesus. Then He, as the mediator of my prayers, carried them to the Father.

The picture seemed pretty ironclad. After all, we are not good enough to go directly to the Father in prayer. Therefore we give our prayers to someone more worthy and He carries them to the Father for us. That's what a mediator is, right? Perhaps in some cases.

I am now absolutely convinced that is not what Paul meant. To correct this picture, let's first back up and take a look at some early prayers. Go back almost 4000 years and look at Abraham's prayer habits.

Prayer and the Altar

In **Genesis 12:8** Abraham moved to the mountain east of Bethel. He pitched his tent, built an altar and called on the name of the Lord.

In **Genesis 13:1-4** he traveled to Egypt because of a famine. When he returned to Canaan, he went back to the place where he built the altar to call on the name of the Lord.

In **Genesis 13:18** Abraham moved by the terebinth trees of Mamre and built another altar to the Lord, presumably to call upon His name again.

Isaac followed his father's example. In **Genesis 26:25** he came to Beersheba, built an altar and called on the name of the Lord.

Jacob continued the family tradition. When he returned to Canaan from his extended stay with Laban, he went to Shechem. In **Genesis 33:20** one of the first things he did after purchasing land was build an altar to the God of Israel.

March through history to King David, who followed the example of his patriarchs. In **I Chronicles 21:26** when God plagued Israel because of the unlawful census, David built an altar and called on the name of the Lord.

Throughout the Old Testament prayer and the altar of sacrifice are interconnected. God sealed that connection in **Isaiah 56:7**: "Even them I will bring to My holy mountain, and make them joyful in My house of prayer. Their burnt offerings and their sacrifices will be accepted on My altar; for My house shall be called a house of prayer for all nations." Why would God accept burnt offerings on the altar in His temple? Because that house was a house of prayer. The altar of sacrifice was needed for prayer and prayer always accompanied the altar of sacrifice.

In reality, the connection between the altar and prayer is common sense. After all, what right do we sinful people have to approach the holy, righteous God and call on His name? Do you remember God's statements in **Isaiah 59:1-2**, "Behold, the Lord's hand is not shortened, that it cannot save; nor his ear heavy that it cannot hear. But your iniquities have separated you from your God; and your sins have hidden His face from you, so that He will not hear."

Sin separates us from God, destroying the fellowship He intended us to have with Him. Our sin keeps Him from heeding our prayers. Amazingly, instead of judging men immediately, God developed a plan by which men could be cleansed of their sins. Once atonement was made, men could approach God in prayer.

According to **Leviticus 17:11** that plan was through blood sacrifice. God said, "For the life of the flesh is in the blood, and I have given it to you upon the altar to make atonement for your souls; for it is the blood that makes atonement for the soul." The blood of an innocent was to be shed. The sacrifice died, bearing the sins of the one offering the sacrifice. The death of the sacrifice was applied to the sinner to cleanse him.

Abraham, Isaac, Jacob and David needed a sacrifice to cleanse their iniquities, reconciling them to the Father, allow-ing them to call on His name. They needed a mediator to bring them into God's presence. The sacrifice was the mediator that allowed them to pray.

Jesus: Our Mediator

Fast forward to the New Testament and learn that the blood of bulls and goats could not ultimately take sins away. **Hebrews 10:1-4**, "For the law...can never with these same sacrifices, which they offer continually year by year, make those who approach perfect...For it is not possible that the blood of bulls and goats could take away sins."

The Old Testament sacrificial system did not really work. Those sacrifices were not really intended to provide the grace we need. Rather, the Old Testament was a teacher to point us to and prepare us for the ultimate sacrifice—God's Son, Jesus. As **Galatians 3:24** says, "The law was our tutor to bring us to Christ that we might be justified by faith."

The Old Testament sacrifices lead us to Christ by prefiguring His sacrifice, which would truly provide forgiveness. Similarly, **Isaiah 53** prophesied that sacrifice. Consider some of the statements made regarding the suffering servant of God who would be exalted:

> ...Surely He has borne our griefs and carried our sorrows...He was wounded for our transgressions; He was bruised for our iniquities; The chastisement for our peace was upon Him; And by His stripes we are healed...And the Lord has laid on Him the iniquity of us all...He was led as a lamb to the slaughter...For the transgressions of My people he was stricken...He bore the sin of many, and made intercession for the transgressors.

Considering these prophecies and the thousands of years of animal sacrifice, we can begin to picture the true force of John the Baptist's statement in **John 1:29**, "Behold! The Lamb of God who takes away the sin of the world!"

Jesus is God's sacrificial lamb to cleanse us and atone for our sins. Through this sacrifice, those who faithfully obeyed, whether under the Old Covenant or the New, were redeemed. **Hebrews 9:13-15** says:

For if the blood of bulls and goats and the ashes of a heifer, sprinkling the unclean, sanctifies for the purifying of the flesh, how much more shall the blood of Christ, who through the eternal Spirit offered Himself without spot to God, cleanse your conscience from dead works to serve the living God? And for this reason He is the Mediator of the new covenant, by means of death, for the redemption of the transgressions under the first covenant, that those who are called may receive the promise of the eternal inheritance.

Suddenly the picture of the only mediator between man and God, the Man Christ Jesus, takes on a new light. Jesus is not the mediator of our prayers because He takes our prayers to the Father. Jesus is the mediator because He "gave Himself a ransom for all" (**I Timothy 2:6**). His ransom redeemed us from our sins, reconciling us to the Father, restoring our fellowship with Him.

In **Romans 6:3-5** Paul said:

Or do you not know that as many of us as were baptized into Christ Jesus were baptized into His death? Therefore we were buried with Him through baptism into death, that just as Christ was raised from the dead by the glory of the Father, even so we also should walk in newness of life. For if we have been united together in the likeness of His death, certainly we also shall be in the likeness of His resurrection.

If we die with Christ in baptism we participate in His death and His sacrifice. **Colossians 1:22** says, "And you, who once were alienated and enemies in your mind by wicked works, yet now He has reconciled in the body of His flesh through death, to present you holy and blameless, and above reproach in His sight." With this reconciliation, Jesus does not take our prayers to the Father; He presents us to the Father holy, blameless and above reproach. Since we have been redeemed by the blood of the Lamb, we can enter the presence of God.

Thus, **Hebrews 10:19-22** says:

Therefore, brethren, having boldness to enter the Holiest by the living blood of Jesus, by a new and living way which He consecrated for us, through the veil, that is, His flesh, and having a High Priest over the house of God, let us draw near with a true heart in full assurance of faith, having our hearts sprinkled from an evil conscience and our bodies washed with pure water.

Because Jesus died as our sacrifice and because we died to sin in Him, we can go directly to the Father in prayer. Jesus is our mediator, not because He takes our prayers to the Father, but because He brings us to the Father. He is the Mediator between God and man.

This book is about prayer. However, perhaps you picked up this book to learn about prayer without having been baptized into Christ's death as **Romans 6:3** taught. Please allow me to encourage you to study **Romans 6** and obey its teaching on baptism. There is no way to approach the Father in prayer but through Christ. **Acts 4:12** said, "Nor is there salvation in any other, for there is no other name under heaven given among men by which we must be saved." Further, in **John 14:6** Jesus said, "I am the way, the truth, and the life. No one comes to the Father except through Me." He is the one and only Mediator between God and man.

Prayer Challenge:

Without Christ's sacrifice there would be no way to pray. List other blessings God granted to us through sacrificing His Son on our behalf.

Consider the freedom we have in Christ. Under the Old Law, to pray, the Israelites had to travel to Jerusalem and sacrifice animals. Today, however, God has offered the sacrifice that grants us that privilege. What other freedoms has God granted us in Christ?

Plug In:

Holy Father in Heaven,

I stand in awe of Your overwhelming lovingkindness. I have no right to be in Your presence, but You offered the sacrifice that allows me here. Thank You.

Help me to ever look to the cross of Your Son, to remember the price paid for my salvation. Strengthen me to conduct myself in a manner befitting that sacrifice.

Please, forgive me my sins. I am sorry that my life led to Your Son's death, but I thank You that You paid the price for me, that Your Son took the stripes that were due me. Thank You for Your grace and mercy.

Thank You for the freedom You have given me in Christ.

I love You.

In Christ's name I pray,

Amen

Plugged In: High Voltage Prayer

Chapter 20

Praying In Jesus' Name

He Forgot To Say It

Though it happened while I was in high school, I remember it as though it were yesterday. There I was, sitting on the second row with the other boys. The worship assembly was being dismissed with prayer by one of my friends, a very spiritually minded young man.

He was nervous and in the middle of his prayer lost his train of thought. Not knowing what to say next, he just ended his prayer with an "Amen."

I saw his dad walk to the front and I knew it was over for my friend. He had ruined the closing prayer. He led us all but it did no good for him or anyone else. He had forgotten to say, "In Jesus' name."

My friend evidently had the same thought. The first thing he said was something like, "I'm sorry, Dad, I got nervous and forgot to say, 'In Jesus' name.'"

Was I ever astonished when his dad responded, "That's alright, Son. Praying in Jesus' name does not mean just saying those words. You did a fine job. Keep up the good work."

What?! How could this be? Every prayer I had ever heard ended with those words—"In Jesus' name we pray, Amen." How could the prayer possibly work if you did not end it with that mantra?

Then one day I read the Sermon on the Mount again and noticed Jesus ended His model prayer without teaching His disciples to say, "In Jesus' name." If I follow the example in **Matthew 6:9-13**, I would end my prayers exactly as my friend did so many years ago—with a simple "Amen."

Why Say It

If Jesus did not teach us to say, "In Jesus' name," when He gave the model prayer, then why do we always say it? We say it because our prayers are to be offered in Jesus' name. According to **Colossians 3:17**, "Whatever you do in word or deed, do all in the name of the Lord Jesus." "Whatever you do" includes praying. Additionally, as Jesus gave further instruction to the disciples in **John 16:23-24**, He instructed them to pray in His name.

Because of these two statements, we end nearly every prayer with the words, "In Jesus' name." After all, we are praying in Jesus' name; why not let everyone know?

164

Do We Have To Say It

Are you ready for a shock? Saying, "In Jesus' name," does not make the prayer in Jesus' name. On the other hand, not saying that phrase does not mean the prayer was not offered in His name.

Despite what some may say, according to the Bible, merely saying the name of Jesus has absolutely no power. Saying Jesus' name does not sanctify our prayers, our baptism or any other action we may take.

Consider the seven sons of Sceva in **Acts 19:13-16**:

Then some of the itinerant Jewish exorcists took it upon themselves to call the name of the Lord Jesus over those who had evil spirits, saying "We exorcise you by the Jesus whom Paul preaches." Also there were seven sons of Sceva, a Jewish chief priest, who did so. And the evil spirit said, "Jesus I know, and Paul I know; but who are you?" Then the man in whom the evil spirit was leaped on them, overpowered them, and prevailed against them, so that they fled out of that house naked and wounded.

They said Jesus' name, but that provided no power to what they were doing. Jesus had given them no power or authority to exorcise demons. Therefore, they could say Jesus' name all day long, but it would do them no good. Performing an action in Jesus' name means we are actually doing something in His name, not that we merely say it is in His name.

Go back to **Colossians 3:17**. Everything we do in word or deed is to be done in Jesus' name. Does that mean we have to say those words before we do everything?

I can imagine it now. "In Jesus' name, I open my eyes. In Jesus' name, I get out of bed. In Jesus' name, I make my bed. In Jesus' name, I type this sentence." That would get a little tedious. Oh how thankful I am that is not what God intended.

What Does It Mean Then?

Acts 4:7 gives us some insight. After Peter and John healed the lame man, the Jewish council asked them, "By what power or by what name have you done this?" In **vs. 10**, they replied, "...by the name of Jesus Christ of Nazareth...this man stands here before you whole."

Notice the connection made in the question, "By what power or by what name...?" Doing something in Jesus' name means doing it by His power. Praying in Jesus' name, then, means praying by Jesus' power.

Consider an illustration. Have you ever watched a cop show in which the police officer pulls his gun and says, "Stop in the name of the law!"? He is declaring that he has been empowered or authorized by the law to command the individual to stop.

When we say we are praying in Jesus' name, we are claiming we are empowered by Jesus Christ to pray. This takes us back to our last chapter. We are empowered to pray because Jesus is our Mediator. We are able to pray because the sacrifice of Jesus empowers us to enter the Holy place and pray to God (**Hebrews 10:19-22**).

Praying What Jesus Wants

Praying in Jesus' name means not only praying because He has authorized us to, but also praying what Jesus has authorized us to pray and in the way He has authorized us to pray.

This is the crux of effective prayer. Prayer is not to be about getting what we want, but aligning our wills with God's. We truly pray in Jesus' name when we are most concerned about Jesus being glorified and His will being done. Our prayer is to follow Jesus' model prayer, wanting God's will to be done in our lives and on earth as it is done in heaven (**Matthew 6:10**).

When I was a kid, I would often ask my dad to do things he did not want to do. "Hey, dad," I would say as we drove home, "can we stop and get an ice cream?" He would respond, "Let's don't, but say we did." You can imagine I did not like that approach very much. I much preferred it when he would take me out for ice cream and tell me that I was not supposed to say anything about it.

Regrettably, too many prayers are offered with the "let's don't, but say we did" mentality. Too many pray without giving much thought to what Jesus wants us to pray. Then they tack on the power phrase "in Jesus' name" and believe they really have prayed in Jesus' name. God would much rather us pray by Jesus' authority without saying so, than pray however we want and then say we prayed in Jesus' name.

We must pray as Jesus has authorized and empowered us to pray. That takes study and growth. That includes all that we have studied already and all that we will study throughout the remaining chapters.

One final thought—I certainly agree it is good to let people know we are praying in Jesus' name by saying so. However, we must not become like the Pharisees and develop an unwritten law that every prayer must end this way just to satisfy our sense of expediency. Let's focus on praying in Jesus' name and not so much on claiming to do so.

Try ending your prayer without this commonly used phrase sometimes. Instead, begin your prayer with it. Or end your prayer saying, "By the power of Jesus" or "By the authority of Jesus." Whatever you do, the important issue is that you actually pray in Jesus' name, not that you say you did.

Prayer Challenge:

Give consideration to your general prayers. What about them makes them in Jesus' name? How would you respond if someone asked you to prove your prayers were really done in Jesus' name?

According to **Hebrews 10:19-25**, the sacrifice of Jesus is what empowers us to enter God's presence in prayer. Give thought to the great blessing Jesus has provided us through His death. Also, what did the Hebrew encourage us to do since Jesus has so empowered us?

Plug In:

Father in heaven,

By the authority of Jesus I enter Your presence.

I thank You for offering the sacrifice that has reconciled me to You. Thank You for sprinkling my heart and removing my evil conscience and washing me of my sins.

Help me to hold fast the confession of my faith without wavering, trusting You to be faithful.

Strengthen me to encourage Your children, my brethren, stirring them up to love and good deeds, assembling with them and encouraging them.

Father, I look forward to the day when I am fully in Your presence.

I love You.

Amen

Group Discussion:

What were the most important lessons you learned about prayer this week?

How did this week's readings help your prayer life?

What advice would you give others based on this week's reading to help them pray?

With what issues do you need help or prayers based on this week's reading?

How can we keep our prayers from being selfish?

List and be prepared to share some of the blessings from God for which you are most thankful?

What do you think most hinders our ability to persist in prayer? How can we overcome these obstacles?

How did Jesus become the Mediator of our prayers? What comfort do you have in being able to go directly to God's presence for prayer?

How do we actually pray in Jesus' name?

Plugged In: High Voltage Prayer

WEEK FIVE

"Likewise the Spirit also helps in our weaknesses. For we do not know what we should pray for as we ought, but the Spirit Himself makes intercession for us with groanings which cannot be uttered. Now He who searches the hearts knows what the mind of the Spirit is, because He makes intercession for the saints according to the will of God."

Romans 8:26-27

Plugged In: High Voltage Prayer

Chapter 21

The Holy Spirit: Intercessor For The Saints

Slow of Speech

Moses was more than a little frightened. First, he encountered a strange burning bush that would not be consumed by the flame. Then he discovered God was calling him from within it. Finally, God was calling him to go back into Egypt, face the Pharaoh and talk him into letting the Israelites go.

Considering he had 40 years of shepherding with which to remember his failed attempt to deliver the Israelites the first time, we can well imagine how distressed this call made him. I am not surprised he came up with all manner of excuses.

In **Exodus 4:10**, Moses said "O my Lord, I am not eloquent, neither before nor since You have spoken to Your servant; but I am slow of speech and slow of tongue."

When God answered this excuse, Moses persisted saying, "O my Lord, please send by the hand of whomever else You may send" (**Exodus 4:13**).

After this, God enlisted Moses' brother Aaron. He would intercede with Pharaoh on Moses' behalf. Where Moses thought he was not eloquent and thought he was slow of speech, he believed Aaron could speak for Him.

Prayer, however, is not about Moses—it is about us. It is not about going to Pharaoh—it is about going to God. If Moses had this fear of speaking to a king, how much more might we have this fear when we are addressing the sovereign ruler of the universe?

But we do not need to fear. God, in His infinite wisdom and mercy, has provided an intercessor for us—His Holy Spirit. When we are not eloquent and are slow of prayer, the Holy Spirit will speak for us.

The Spirit: Our Sanctifier

The passage that comforts us, assuring us that the Holy Spirit intercedes on our behalf is **Romans 8:26-27**:

Likewise the Spirit also helps in our weaknesses. For we do not know what we should pray for as we ought, but the Spirit Himself makes intercession for us with groanings which cannot be uttered. Now He who searches the hearts knows what the mind of the Spirit is, because He makes intercession for the saints according to the will of God.

However, before we examine that passage directly, we will look at its context.

In **vss. 12-15**, Paul demonstrated that the help of the Spirit began when He brought us into close relationship with the Father. We who are led by the Spirit, whose minds are focused on the things of the Spirit and not the things of the flesh, are sons of God. We have received the Spirit of adoption.

According to **Ephesians 1:5-6**, this adoption has made us accepted by God in the Beloved. This is a very intimate picture of the sanctifying work of the Holy Spirit. According to **II Thessalonians 2:13**, we are chosen for salvation "through sanctification by the Spirit and belief in the truth." When we believe the truth, the Spirit sets us apart, sanctifying us as the sons of God.

According to Paul in **Romans 8:15**, it is because we are set apart by the Spirit in adoption that we may cry out to God in prayer saying, "Abba, Father." Evidently, this term "Abba" was a very special term to the Jews. While some slaves might have been considered so close to their master as to call the master, Father, they could never use this very special term, "Abba." This term was reserved in use for actual children. Through the Spirit, we really are God's children.

The Spirit's work in our prayers began the moment He sanctified us through our belief in the truth. Jesus' sacrifice paid the price for our redemption and reconciliation. The Spirit's sanctification set us apart as holy vessels useful to the Master. Because He sanctified us, making us holy, we can approach the Holy God in prayer as His children.

The Spirit: Our Witness

Only those who have been sprinkled clean by the blood of the Lamb can enter the presence of God. Only those who are adopted through sanctification of the Spirit can cry out, "Abba, Father."

How does God know we are His children? Certainly, we could say, "God knows." However, Paul added this further assurance by stating that the Holy Spirit bears witness along with our spirit that we are children of God (**Romans 8:16**).

As Paul said in **Ephesians 1:13**, when we trusted God, having believed His word, we were sealed with the Holy Spirit. This seal is like a king's seal on a letter proving the document is his. The Holy Spirit sanctifies us and, along with our spirit, confesses our sonship to God.

Thus, the Holy Spirit speaks on our behalf to the Father, proclaiming our privilege to address Him as His children because only His children can truly address Him in prayer. The Spirit, as our witness, is the seal that says the King, Jesus, has sent us holy and blameless to speak to the Father.

The Spirit: Our Intercessor

The above was important because Paul begins **Romans 8:26** saying, "Likewise the Spirit also helps in our weaknesses." That is, just as He sanctifies us and bears witness on our behalf, He helps our weaknesses.

How does He help our weaknesses? There are many times when we are slow of speech and slow of tongue. We need somebody to speak eloquently for us to our King. The Spirit does that.

There are times when we do not know what to pray. Perhaps through immaturity we do not yet know exactly how to pray or even what we should pray for. In those cases, the Spirit intercedes on our behalf, perfecting what lacks.

Perhaps we face a difficult situation and we just simply do not know what we should pray for. This is often the case when we pray for someone who is extremely ill. The disease might leave them incapacitated if they do not die, but who knows what they might accomplish if they live. We do not know what to pray. The Holy Spirit does and He intercedes for us.

Perhaps we are not sure what God would want in any given situation. We want God's will to be done but we do not know how to pray for it because we are not certain what it is. The Spirit does, and He intercedes on our behalf.

This intercession is, no doubt, the great comfort that keeps us praying even when we know we really do not know what we are doing. It is the encouragement that keeps us praying when we realize we really have no right to be here.

The Spirit has sanctified us, setting us apart for adoption. As we approach the Father, the Spirit testifies that we are God's children. Finally, when we are standing there stuttering, mumbling and unsure what we should say, The Spirit takes up our plea and prays on our behalf, interceding for us.

How great our God is.

Prayer Challenge:

Have any excuses kept you from praying? If so, list them below and realize the Spirit is our intercessor. He overcomes our excuses. Pray anyway.

Consider the numerous way in which we need help from God. List some below and ponder how awesome and merciful our God is to provide the help we need.

Plug In:

Abba, Father,

Holy and reverend is Your name.

Please forgive me of my sins, cleansing me and reconciling me to You.

Thank You for granting Your Spirit to work on my behalf. So often I do not know what to pray and even when I do know, my ability is limited.

Father, I pray that Your will be done here on earth. Sanctify me, cleanse me and use me as Your instrument to accomplish Your work. I pray that I will be useful to You.

For the sacrifice of Your Son, You are worthy of praise, glory and honor. Holy, holy, holy are You Lord Most High.

I love You.

By Jesus' authority I pray,

Amen

Chapter 22

The Prayer Of Adoration

Sacrifice Of Praise

"You also, as living stones, are being built up a spiritual house, a holy priesthood, to offer up spiritual sacrifices acceptable to God through Jesus Christ" (**I Peter 2:5**).

What kind of sacrifices are spiritual sacrifices? **Hebrews 13:15** says, "Let us continually offer the sacrifice of praise to God, that is, the fruit of our lips, giving thanks to His name."

One sacrifice is praise with thanksgiving. No wonder Peter went on to say in **I Peter 2:9**, "But you are...a royal priesthood...that you may proclaim the praises of Him who called you out of darkness into His marvelous light."

We are sacrificing the time we use to honor God. More than that, in order to praise God, we must sacrifice our own pride. We praise God because we recognize His power over us. In order to give thanks, we must sacrifice our own self-sufficiency. When we thank God, we state we were in need and God provided for us what we could not provide for ourselves.

Let us continually sacrifice the fruit of our lips to God.

Thanksgiving and Praise

To distinguish praise from thanksgiving, we can say thanksgiving adores God for what He has already done. Though at times, we may offer thanks for what we are utterly convinced God will do. Praise adores God for what He is and what He can do.

Of course, we can quote numerous scriptures that direct us to thank and praise God (see **Hebrews 13:15; I Peter 2:5, 9** above). However, this command is really only the smallest of reasons for which the Christian adores God.

In fact, if there were no Bible commands to adore and honor God, the one whose mind is focused on the things of the Spirit would praise and thank God anyway. Adoration is not just an act of worship to mark off our checklist. In reality, it is the natural response to God from the saint who knows how awesome God is.

Just take stock of all God has done. We begin in the beginning. He created the heavens and the earth. He sustains the universe at all times. He has established the days and the seasons. He causes the sun to shine and the rain to fall. He created a nation from a single family. Through that family He brought us a Savior. He revealed His will through His Holy Spirit. He established His church to strengthen us.

All this just hits some of the major highlights and none of it hits on what He has done for us individually.

In the end, we realize we adore God with praise and thanksgiving, not because we have to, but because He deserves it. As the Psalmist said in **Psalm 96:8**, "Give to the Lord the glory due His name." As the elders in **Revelation 4:11** said, "You are worthy, O Lord, to receive glory and honor and power."

God is worthy of praise and thanksgiving, so we who are in awe of Him naturally respond with adoration.

We Need To Adore God

As we learned about prayer in general, we must remember about praise and thanksgiving in specific. We do not adore God because He needs it. Remember **Psalm 50:10-12**. If He needed something, He would not ask us.

We adore God because we need it.

Praise and thanksgiving consistently remind us who God is and who we are. **Psalm 50:21** demonstrates how wrong it is to think God is like us: "You thought that I was altogether like you; but I will rebuke you, and set them in order before your eyes." Blessing God reminds us of who and what God is and what He has done and can do. It reminds us God is not at all like us. Interestingly, a common means of praise in the Psalms is to question "who is like God?" If we consistently honor God as God, we will not falter, thinking He is like us.

Praise and thanksgiving awaken our dependence upon God and uplift our confidence in Him. Of course, we could also say our dependence upon and confidence in God awaken praise and thanksgiving. It is a cycle.

Psalm 71 demonstrates this. The psalmist knew he could trust God because of what God had done in the past. If the psalmist never took the time to praise and thank God, he would lose sight of all God had done.

Finally, praise and thanksgiving help us maintain the proper perspective on our lives. A regular habit of adoration reminds us what God has done for us, taking our minds off what we wanted from Him that He has not yet done or might not do.

With our improved perspective, adoration strengthens the other aspects of our prayers. Confession becomes more humble, fervent and confident. Supplication is less self-centered and more centered upon God and others.

Practicing Adoration

When we come into the presence of God and want to adore Him, how do we do it?

First, the foundation for all of this is to actually adore God. We will only verbalize our adoration when our hearts are truly filled with awe and gratitude. As **I Peter 3:15** says, we must sanctify God in our hearts. That is, we must value and adore Him above all other things.

As you verbalize your adoration, don't just think about the physical blessings. Those are great, but the spiritual blessings in Christ are greater. In **Ephesians 1:3** Paul said, "Blessed be the God and Father of our Lord Jesus Christ, who has blessed us with every spiritual blessing in the heavenly places in Christ."

Honor God for something. Don't just give thanks and praise for "the many physical and spiritual blessings." Adore God for something specific. Look at **Psalm 104** as an example. The psalmist specifically praised God for laying the foundations of the earth, for sending springs of water into the valleys to quench the thirst of the wild beasts, for giving homes to the birds, for growing grass for the cattle and vegetation for man to have food. We need to adore God for something.

Bless God for everything. Do not think the big things are so obvious you do not need to verbalize them. On the other hand, do not overlook the small things. Listen to your children pray as they thank God for everything from the sunlight to their nightlight, from their home to their bedroom to their tennis shoes.

If you are struggling with exactly how to word your praise and thanksgiving, verbalize scripture. For instance, "Not unto us, O Lord, not unto us, but to Your name give glory, because of your mercy, because of your truth. Why should the Gentiles say, 'So where is their God?' But our God is in heaven; He does whatever He pleases" (**Psalm 115:1-3**).

Finally, just do it. Our God is worthy of blessing, honor, glory, praise and thanksgiving. We need to give Him His due.

In some prayers, just offer adoration. Praise God for who He is and what He can do. Thank God for what He has done. Leave your requests for another prayer. Just adore God for a few minutes. You will be amazed at how it changes your perspective on nearly every aspect of your day.

Prayer Challenge:

Make a list of issues for which you can praise, thank and adore God. Then simply pray a prayer of adoration.

What about God makes Him so worthy of our adoration?

Plug In:

Father in Heaven,

Hallowed be Your name.

You, O Lord, who created and sustain all things, are magnificent beyond my comprehension. You have created not only the universe and all it contains, but also my deliverance and salvation.

I thank You because Your lovingkindness is everlasting. You have granted me life, health and strength, but more than that, You have granted me life in Your Son.

By Your grace and might I have a place to live. I eat every day. I have clothes to wear. You have given me a family, both physically and spiritually. You have blessed me with the beauty of Your world.

Your grace and power are overwhelming and I praise and thank You.

I love you.

By Jesus' power I pray,

Amen

Chapter 23

The Prayer Of Confession

Why Confess?

You may be wondering why Christians need to confess their sins at all. After all, Jesus died to forgive our sins. All of our sins were in the future from Jesus' standpoint on the cross. Does it not stand to reason that when we were baptized for the remission of our sins (**Acts 2:38**) Jesus forgave all of them?

Let's let the Bible answer that question.

First, Jesus taught us to confess our sins and seek forgiveness when He taught how to pray in the kingdom in **Matthew 5:12**. "Forgive us our debts," He said.

Further, in **Romans 6:23** Paul explained the wages of sin are death. He was writing to Christians about their sins after turning to the Lord. Therefore, when we turn to sin after our baptism, we earn death again. We need to confess our sin to God and seek His forgiveness.

We can be grateful God is faithful to forgive us our sins when we confess them, as John said in **I John 1:8-9**. This, of course, may have been a sticking point for us. We may have feared our sins were too much to be forgiven; especially since we sinned when we knew better.

However, we remember God already knew all of the sins we would commit in our entire lives. Yet He sent His Son to be the propitiation for our sins anyway. Why hold back on confession? God already knows what we have done. Let's just admit it and make a clean slate of it.

Finally, confession is not only good for the soul, it is good for the body. As we hold back, our mounting guilt can cause all kinds of stress. That stress can in turn affect our body. We can lose sleep. We can make ourselves sick. David expressed this in **Psalm 32:3-4**, "When I kept silent, my bones grew old through my groaning all the day long. For day and night Your hand was heavy upon me; my vitality was turned into the drought of summer." When David confessed, God forgave Him.

"Why should we confess?" you may ask. Those sound like good reasons to me.

God Glorifying Confession

When Achan sinned by keeping some of the bounty from defeated Jericho, Joshua told him to "give glory to the Lord God of Israel, and make confession to Him" (**Joshua 7:19**). How does confession glorify God?

First, consider what confession really is. The word translated "confess" literally means to speak the same words. Confessing sin to God means to say the same thing about our sins that God says about them. Confession glorifies God because it says, "You are right, God, here is the truth about me and my sins."

Read Daniel's confession to God in **Daniel 9:4-19** and David's confessions in **Psalm 32** and **51**. Consider the following lessons we learn about confession from these examples.

Confession glorifies God by acknowledging God's holiness. Further, confession acknowledges we need God's grace if we are going to be holy like Him.

As David did, we acknowledge and glorify God's justice for judging our sins and also His mercy for forgiving them.

Finally, when we confess our sins to God we acknowledge He is the lawgiver and His laws are the standard. After all, sin is lawlessness (**I John 3:4**). Whose law are we disobeying? God's. In an age where most want to follow their own standard, confession truly glorifies God.

Practicing Confession

As we confess, we must recognize what sin means. Sin is not a mistake, an indiscretion or a character flaw. Sin is rebellion against God. It is lawlessness. Finally, even for us, God's children, sin means separation and death. **Isaiah 59:2** says, "But your iniquities have separated you from your God; and your sins, have hidden His face from you." **Romans 6:23** says, "The wages of sin is death."

The publican fully understood the impact of his sins in **Luke 18:13**. He did not come to God with excuses or justifications. He did not try to mitigate his sinfulness by reminding

God about how sinful everyone else was too. He just said, "God, be merciful to me a sinner."

Be honest with yourself and with God. If you took the Lord's name in vain, do not confess a slip of the tongue; confess blasphemy. If you lusted, do not confess a wandering eye; confess adultery in your heart. If you blew up at your husband or wife, do not confess that your spouse ticked you off; confess your lack of self-control.

As with all aspects of prayer, be specific. Regrettably, the average Christian does little more confessing than, "Forgive us of our sins." At the very least, that is often the extent of confession in corporate worship. Look at some of the confessions in scripture. Read the confession in **Daniel 9** again. Read **Ezra 9** and **Nehemiah 9**. These confessions were specific.

Remember confession means saying the same thing about our sins that God says about them. God says so much more than just, "You are sinners." We must be specific and say what these specific sins really mean. I know that salvation does not hinge upon perfectly complete confession any more than it hinges on perfect living. However, if we are going to confess, truly confess, we will lay out our specific sins before God.

Specific confession helps us more than it helps God. I can remember when I realized that I never mentioned any specifics in my confessions. I prayed every night for God to forgive me, but I never gave any thought to what sins I really needed forgiven. Therefore, I never gave any thought to what I was going to do the next day to keep from committing them again, which leads us to our next point.

If we want forgiveness, we must do more than confess, say we are sorry and ask for forgiveness. According to **Proverbs 28:13**, we must not cover our sins; instead we must confess them and forsake them. We must repent, turning away from our sins in order to be forgiven.

Finally, for confession to be effective, we must be willing to forgive those who sin against us. We come full circle back to Jesus' teaching on confession in **Matthew 6:12**. "Forgive us our debts, as we forgive our debtors." Jesus went on to say in **vs. 14-15** that God will forgive us only if we forgive others.

We must never take confession for granted. Instead, we must remember David's words in **Psalm 32**. "Blessed is he whose transgression is forgiven, whose sin is covered." We are indeed blessed. However, we will be blessed only if we confess.

Prayer Challenge:

In **Ezra 10:1**, Ezra was weeping while he confessed. In **Psalm 32**, David spoke of the blessing of forgiveness. What kind of emotions go along with the prayer of confession?

Are there any sins you have been covering? God already knows them and has already sent His Son to die for them. Confess those right now and forsake them. Be honest and specific.

Plug In:

Holy Father in Heaven,

I am too ashamed and humiliated to lift up my face to You, my God; for my iniquities have risen higher than my head and my guilt has grown up to the heavens.

Be merciful to me a sinner. I have fallen short of Your holiness. I need Your grace. I am unworthy of Your favor. You are justified in judging and condemning me for I have been wicked in Your sight.

Father, forgive me my trespasses. Forgive my impure thoughts and actions. Forgive my pride and my immorality. Forgive me for the lawlessness I have committed and the devotion I have omitted.

Help me know my sins and turn from them. Please, forgive me the sins I have committed in ignorance and help me to understand Your will.

Thank You for Your Son's blood, the propitiation for my sins. Thank You, Father, for Your word, revealed by Your Spirit, that has told me how to have forgiveness in Your Son.

Thank You for forgiving me. I will praise You in the congregation for Your lovingkindness is everlasting.

I love You.

Through Your Son I pray,

Amen

Chapter 24

The Prayer Of Supplication

Petition and Intercession

Dietrich Bonhoeffer claimed "the essence of Christian prayer is not general adoration, but specific concrete petition." How can this be? How can it be that an all-powerful, all-knowing, all-holy God allows us to ask Him to work on our pitiful behalf?

What is more amazing is that He allows us to supplicate on behalf of others, to intercede as though we are close friends who get to bend His ear. What a magnificent Father we have.

Mistaken Concepts

Supplication is not our genie in the bottle. We do not get our every desire just by rubbing the magic prayer lamp. **Matthew 6:10** says, "Your will be done on earth as it is in heaven." Even our supplication should not be done to accomplish our will, but God's. This governs everything else we learn about prayer. Our overriding concern must be that God be glorified and His will be done.

When Moses interceded for Israel in **Exodus 32:11-14**, the prayer was about God's glory, not Israel's salvation. In **Psalm 74**, Asaph prayed for Judah's deliverance but the reason was that God would be glorified.

Supplication is not spiritual manipulation. God explained in **Isaiah 43:13** that He works and we cannot reverse it. We cannot pressure God to do our will. We may simply ask Him to take our prayer into account.

Oddly enough, while I was working on this chapter at home, two of my children walked up behind me with smiles on their faces and asked, "So that we won't bug you, may we please watch a movie." Now that is manipulation. My sweet, adorable little children were hoping to get what they wanted by making it sound like it was all for me. We must not supplicate God like this. We must truly desire God's glory and God's will, not just try to gain what we want by making it sound like it is good for God also.

Supplication is not acceptable whining. Too often our request prayers are laundry lists of complaints regarding what God has not done. Instead, we must remember what God has done. That is why **Philippians 4:6-7** says our requests should be made with thanksgiving. Despite the clichéd joke that whining is a little known form of prayer, just as we do not appreciate whining from our children, God does not appreciate it from His.

Finally, supplication is not FGI (For God's Information). We are not informing God of our needs and wants when we pray. **Matthew 6:8** says God knows what we need before we even ask Him.

Why Supplicate?

He has invited us to do so. **I Peter 5:7** says, "[cast] all your care upon Him, for He cares for you." This is an amazing thought all by itself.

While this may surprise you, supplication invites God to act. **James 4:2** says, "You do not have because you do not ask." Additionally, in **Ezekiel 22:30-31**, all God wanted was someone who would stand in the gap and intercede for Israel. No one would, so God judged her. How many of God's gifts have gone unreceived simply because no one asked?

Supplication humbles us and glorifies God, demonstrating our need for God's powerful hand in our lives. We need what God has to give, because every good gift comes from Him (**James 1:17**).

When we ask for physical blessings, we recognize our physical limitations. When we pray for spiritual blessings, we recognize how much we need God's mercy. When we intercede for others, we demonstrate that we, as strong and as able as we might be, cannot provide what they need. Only God can.

Finally, we ask God, because asking works. As **James 5:16** explains, "The effective, fervent prayer of a righteous man avails much." Even when I am not completely sure how prayer works, I can rest assured that true prayer does work.

For What And Whom

I Timothy 2:1 is pretty plain. We are to pray for all men, including brethren (**Ephesians 6:18-20**), those in government (**I Timothy 2:2**) and even our enemies (**Matthew 5:44-45**).

What often surprises people, however, is for what we are allowed to pray. We know we are allowed to pray for spiritual needs and blessings. Surely we can pray for forgiveness and salvation (**Matthew 6:12; Romans 10:1**). We can pray for spiritual strength and wisdom (**Colossians 1:9-11; Ephesians 3:14-19**). We can pray for the spread of the gospel (**Ephesians 6:18-20**).

Were you aware we are allowed to pray for physical needs as well? Jesus taught us to pray for our daily bread (**Matthew 6:11**). Further, John prayed that brethren have good physical health and material prosperity (**III John 2**).

Of course we can pray for our physical *needs*. Were you aware we are even allowed to pray for our wants? That is what Paul did in **II Corinthians 12:7-10**. He wanted the thorn in the flesh removed. Therefore he prayed.

Practicing Supplication

As we noted in an earlier chapter, **James 4:3** demonstrates we must ask from pure, selfless motives. We must not be selfish.

We must not limit our supplication to, "Please grant us physical and spiritual blessings." Be specific. This opens our eyes to the specifics for which we need God's power. Many general prayers are space fillers instead of real requests. "God heal the sick the world over." What are we asking here? Unless we believe there is a possibility that God will actually heal every sick person in the world, we are really just filling space. Be specific.

Especially regarding intercession, we must learn to be observant. Many Christians will not tell us their needs. We need to keep our eyes open to their needs in order to intercede on their behalf.

I once heard of a man sitting on the subway who prayed for God to provide a seat for the pregnant woman standing in front of him. After a few minutes, it struck him that he was sitting on the answer to his prayer. As **James 2:14-16** demonstrates we need to ask with the view to be God's tool to grant our requests.

Lastly, and this may seem too obvious—we must ask. While we do not want to take petition and intercession for granted, we must not be ashamed to ask God either. He has granted this grace to us. Further, we must not be the kind of Christian that promises to intercede for someone and then forgets to ever do so. If we are going to supplicate God, we must do it. Remember that **Ephesians 3:20** says God "is able to exceedingly abundantly above all that we ask or think." That means we not only need to ask and think; we need to ask and think big.

Prayer Challenge:

For most of us, requests are the largest part of our prayers. That being the case, we need to make sure our motivation for prayer is proper. What should our motivations be? Do yours need to change? If so, how?

Take a mental look at your brethren (or you might even talk to some of them). What needs do they have and how can God help them? Intercede on their behalf right now.

Plug In:

Almighty Father,

Thank You for listening to my prayer and heeding my voice. You have delivered me from the enemy and cleansed me of my iniquity. I will ever praise You for Your lovingkindness.

Please continue to bless me as You have over the past years. You have given me far more than I deserve. Please grant me food every day. Continue to provide for my body's needs and the needs of my family. Thank You.

More importantly, grant me wisdom and understanding. Help me walk close to You, living according to Your will.

I pray that You will bless my brethren. Grant them health and prosperity, Father. Further, give them wisdom and strength to live for You.

Help me serve You. Your will be done in my life.

I love You.

In Your Son's name I pray,

Amen

Chapter 25

Prayer Postures

Bible Prayer Postures

You may be surprised to learn people in the Bible prayed in numerous postures.

According to **I Kings 19:4**, Elijah sat underneath a "broom tree" and prayed God take his life. In **I Chronicles 17:16**, David sat before the Lord to pray.

I hope I am not speculating too much here, but since King Hezekiah was near death, I assume he was lying down when he prayed in **II Kings 20:2** with his face turned toward the wall.

In **I Kings 18:42** Elijah bowed down with his face between his knees. The NASB says he crouched.

The publican in **Luke 18:13** was standing. However, he refused to look up and, while praying his brief prayer, beat upon his chest.

According to **I Timothy 2:8**, men were to lift holy hands to God in prayer. David mentioned that regarding his prayers as well. In **Psalm 63:4**, he said he would lift up his hands in God's name. Then **Psalm 134:1-2** said the people were to bless God in the sanctuary while lifting their hands to Him.

One of the most common postures of prayer was to kneel. In **Luke 22:41** Jesus knelt down to pray. In **Acts 7:60** Stephen knelt to pray as he was being stoned. Peter knelt when Tabitha was raised from the dead in **Acts 9:40**. Paul knelt down with the Ephesian elders (**Acts 20:36**) and with the disciples in Tyre (**Acts 21:5**).

In **Ezra 9:5-6** Ezra knelt down, but was too humiliated to look up. His head was bowed. However, at the same time, he spread his hands out toward God to pray to Him.

Finally, another prayer posture was lying prostrate. Moses and Jesus both prayed in this manner (**Deuteronomy 9:25; Matthew 26:39**). This might entail being on our knees and bending over until our faces touch the ground. At times, it might mean being laid out flat with our faces to the ground. This kind of posture is not Muslim, it is Biblical.

Does Posture Matter?

I am sure you are wondering why we have read about all these Bible postures.

First, we must notice that God never mandated a particular prayer posture. We can pray with whatever posture we deem best suited to our prayer.

I once read of three preachers discussing prayer while a telephone repairman worked nearby.

The first preacher said, "Kneeling is definitely the best way to pray."

"No," one of the others contended, "I get the best results when I stand with my hands outstretched to heaven."

The third responded, "You are both wrong. The most effective posture is lying face down on the floor."

The repairman could contain himself no longer and said, "Hey fellas, the best prayin' I ever done was the other day when I was hangin' upside down from a telephone pole."

I have prayed while lying in bed, standing in the shower, running in my neighborhood, driving to work, kneeling in my closet, sitting on a bench, standing behind a microphone, holding hands with my family, with my eyes closed, with my eyes open, looking down, looking up and on the list could go.

God is not nearly so concerned about our posture as He is about our prayers.

Whole Body Prayer

However, the second reason for this survey of Bible prayer postures is to notice that many of the great saints who prayed in the Bible did not just pray in their minds. Prayer was a whole body activity for them. These postures were not arbitrary but were a physical representation of what they were expressing in their hearts to God.

Elijah sat under the tree because he was exhausted— mentally, physically and spiritually.

The early saints lifted holy hands to God in blessing evidently as an expression of openness to God. Further, it expressed a sense of reaching out to God in prayer, just as we might hold our hands outstretched to someone we are preparing to hug. Of course, another purpose was to show their hands to God as holy.

The publican looked down and beat his breast because it was the natural expression of his unworthiness. The posture fit the prayer. He would not use the "lifting up holy hands" posture because he knew his hands were full of sin.

Most often the concept of kneeling in the Bible dealt with being in the presence of a great authority. Therefore, Jesus, Stephen and Paul knelt as a demonstration of reverence to God. They recognized the authority of God and knelt before Him.

Prostration could express multiple aspects of prayer. On one hand, as we talk about "hitting our knees" to represent a burden that crushes us down to the point that "all we can do is pray," just so Jesus fell on His face in prayer out of that same sense of burden. On the other hand, like kneeling, prostration is a representation of honor and worship, humbling one's self to the point of being completely on the ground in the presence of another as Moses did when interceding for Israel.

If we really wanted to get into whole body prayer, we could talk about fasting. We could also look at the despair and mourning demonstrated by putting on sackcloth and sitting in ashes. Or we could examine the prayers when people would tear their robes or pull out their hair.

However, what we learn from the Bible is that prayer is not just a mental activity. For some it was also physical as they put not only their whole heart into what they were praying, but also their bodies.

If you want to expand the practical nature of your prayers, put your whole body into it. Are you praying a prayer of joy and blessing to God? Then look heavenward and lift holy hands to God. Are you praying a prayer of contrition and confession? Then look downward and beat your breast with humility. Are you honoring and praising God? Then kneel or lay prostrate in his presence.

I have no doubt taking any of these actions while praying might feel odd at first. However, I am equally certain they will help deepen your prayers as has been the case for me.

Prayer Challenge:

Do you ever have trouble falling asleep while you pray—especially when praying at bedtime? Have you ever thought that might have something to do with what you are doing with you body while praying? Did you fall asleep because you were laying in bed while praying? How will making prayer a whole body activity focus your attention on your prayers better?

Even if you don't want to make a habit of it, at least let your prayers be a whole body experience today. Are you praying a prayer of joy and blessing to God? Then look heavenward and lift your hands to God in prayer. Are you praying a prayer of confession? Then look downward and beat your breast in humility? Are you honoring and praising God? Then kneel or lay prostrate in His presence. Offer a prayer with your whole body right now.

Plug In:

Father in heaven,

I humbly kneel in Your presence. Your power is beyond my comprehension and You are worthy of glory, honor, praise, blessing and power.

As I come into Your presence, I know I am unworthy even to look on Your face. Father, I beat my breast for I am a sinner. Please be merciful to me.

Forever I will bless You and lift my hands in Your name because of the joy You have granted me through Your salvation. Because Your lovingkindness is better than life, I will praise You.

I love You,

By Jesus' authority I pray,

Amen

Group Discussion:

What were the most important lessons you learned about prayer this week?

How did this week's readings help your prayer life?

What advice would you give others based on this week's reading to help them pray?

With what issues do you need help or prayers based on this week's reading?

How does the Holy Spirit intercede for us in prayer?

Why does God deserve our adoration and why do we need to adore God in prayer?

What are the benefits to our spiritual life of proper confession in prayer?

Does it amaze you that God allows us to petition Him and even to intercede on behalf of others? Why?

How do you think varying prayer postures help deepen our prayer experiences?

Plugged In: High Voltage Prayer

210

Week Six

"Our Father in heaven,
Hallowed be Your name.
Your kingdom come.
Your will be done
On earth as it is in heaven.
Give us this day our daily bread.
And forgive us our debts
As we forgive our debtors.
And do not lead us into temptation,
But deliver us from the evil one.
For Your is the kingdom and the power and the glory
forever.
Amen."

Matthew 6:9-13

Chapter 26

Singing As Prayer

The Battle Belongs To The Lord

The outlook was bleak. Three kingdoms had joined together to attack Jehoshaphat and Israel. Jehoshaphat took the greatest and most effective recourse, he prayed to God in the presence of all Judah. Then the Spirit of the Lord filled Jahaziel, a Levite, and declared God would deliver Judah and they would not even have to fight.

Based upon the promise, Jehoshaphat developed an extremely odd battle plan. Jehoshaphat and his army left Jerusalem the following morning to meet the enemy.

II Chronicles 20:21-22 says:

And when he had consulted with the people, he appointed those who should sing to the Lord, and who should praise the beauty of holiness, as they went out before the army and were saying: "Praise the Lord, for His mercy endures forever." Now when they began to sing and to praise, the Lord set ambushes against the people of Ammon, Moab, and Mount Seir, who had come against Judah; and they were defeated.

Who knew that singing could be so powerful? But what was really going on here? Were they just singing? No, these songs were prayers of praise and thanksgiving. As they sang those prayers, or prayed those songs, God worked on their behalf. Talk about Praying Warriors!

More Than Just Praises

Even though we often speak about praising God in song, few Christians regard praising God in song as prayer. Rest assured, that is exactly what it is.

The very first song mentioned in the Bible is a prayer of praise in **Exodus 15:1**, "Then Moses and the children of Israel sang this song _to_ the Lord, and spoke, saying: 'I will sing to the Lord, for he has triumphed gloriously'" (*Emphasis mine-elc).*

The Israelites had just been delivered from Pharaoh by way of the Red Sea. They prayed their thanksgiving and their praises to God in song.

Deborah and Barak did the same thing in **Judges 5:1-31**. "Hear, O kings! Give ear, O princes! I, even I, will sing to the Lord; I will sing praise to the Lord God of Israel."

The psalms repeatedly speak of singing praises to God. Consider **Psalm 9**, "I will praise You, O Lord, with my whole heart; I will tell of all Your marvelous works. I will be glad and rejoice in You; I will sing praise to Your name, O Most High."

No doubt, after this is explained, we can easily see these songs of praise as prayer in song, but what about petitioning God, interceding on behalf of others or confessing? Can we sing those prayers?

The Old Testament psalmists certainly believed so.

David was interceding on behalf of others when he sang, "Let all those who seek You rejoice and be glad in You; and let those who love Your salvation say continually, 'Let God be magnified!'" (**Psalm 70:4**).

Clearly, he was petitioning God when he sang, "Hear a just cause, O Lord, attend to my cry; give ear to my prayer which is not from deceitful lips, let my vindication come from Your presence; let Your eyes look on the things that are right" (**Psalm 17:1-2**).

Further, David was confessing his sins when he sang:

Have mercy upon me, O God, according to Your lovingkindness; according to the multitude of Your tender mercies, blot out my transgressions. Wash me thoroughly from my iniquity, and cleanse me from my sin. For I acknowledge my transgressions, and my sin is always before me. Against You, You only, have I sinned, and done what is evil in Your sight. (Psalm 51:1-4)

Where does this lead us? First, it leads us to recognize what we are doing with a lot of the songs we already sing. We are praying to God in song. That should be taken seriously. We must not just mouth the words and let our minds wander. **Psalm 138:1** says we should sing praises with our whole heart—we are praying, not filling time.

Second, if there is a song that mirrors the praise, thanksgiving, petition or confession in your heart, then sing it to God as a prayer. Or incorporate it in your prayers. When you have family prayer times or group prayer times, find songs that coincide with your prayers that you can sing/pray together.

Third, if you have songwriting abilities, why not write songs of prayer, whether adoration, supplication or confession that your brethren can sing to God? What a great way to use the abilities God has given you.

Consider These Songs

Let's face it. As odd as singing a prayer may sound to you, you have probably been praying in song for years and just not realized it.

Have you ever sung, "Holy, holy, holy, Lord God Almighty! Early in the morning our song shall rise to Thee..."?

Or perhaps you have prayed, "Then sings my soul, my Savior God to Thee; How great Thou art, how great Thou art!"

Or maybe you have confessed, "I'm the one who shouted 'crucify,' I'm the one who made His cross so high, I'm the one who stood and watched Him die; What have I done? I'm the one."

Surely you have petitioned God singing, "Abide with me! Fast falls the eventide, the darkness deepens, Lord, with me abide! When other helpers fail, and comforts flee, help of the helpless, O abide with me!"

If you have sung any of these songs, you have prayed in song. In fact, if you have ever sung a song that ends with "Amen," you were most likely singing a prayer.

What a great way to pray to our God. No wonder James said, "Is anyone cheerful? Let him sing psalms" (**James 5:13**).

Prayer Challenge:

Think about all the songs you sing that are prayers and how they correspond with the prayers you often pray on your own. How can you make them part of your personal prayer life?

Why not sing a prayer right now. Think of a song that mirrors the prayer in your heart and sing it in conjunction with your prayer. Try this in your family prayer time as well.

Plug In:

Father in heaven,

I praise You, O God. For the Son of Your Love. I Praise You, O God, For Your Spirit of Light.

Father, hear the prayer I offer that I may ever live my life courageously. Be my strength in hours of weakness. In my wanderings be my guide. Through endeavor, failure, danger, Father, be at my side.

I need You every hour, most gracious Lord. Be with me, I cannot live without you. I dare not try to take one step alone.

Lord and Father of mankind, forgive my foolish ways; reclothe me in my rightful mind. Forgive my foolish follies and fleshly lures to sin, for I repent in sorrow and strive Your praise to win.

Lead me gently home, Father, when life's toils are ended, and parting days have come. Lest I fall upon the wayside, lead me gently home.

Father, I love You.

In Jesus' name,

Amen

Chapter 27

Praying For God's Will

If It's His Will, Why Pray?

We know we are to pray for God's will. In **Matthew 6:10**, Jesus instructed us to pray, "Your will be done on earth as it is in heaven."

Perhaps the biggest questions we have about prayer center upon praying for God's will. We wonder, if it was God's will, wouldn't He do it any way? And if it is not His will, what good does it do to pray for it?

The big problem here is a misunderstanding of God's will. As we survey the Bible, we see three differing concepts we may refer to as God's will.

Purposed Will

Some things God plans to do and will accomplish no matter what we do or pray. Examine **Acts 2:23** and **4:27-28**.

*Him, being delivered by the determined purpose and fore-knowledge of God, you have taken by lawless hands, have crucified, and put to death (**Acts 2:23**).*

*For truly against Your holy Servant Jesus, whom You anointed, both Herod and Pontius Pilate, with the Gentiles and the people of Israel, were gathered together to do what-ever Your hand and Your purpose determined before to be done (**Acts 4:27-28**).*

God had a plan for saving man. He was going to work it out and no one could stop it. Whatever men or Satan did, God simply incorporated it, using it to accomplish His plan anyway.

I call this God's *Purposed Will*. While not every event is an extension of God's plans, some are. For instance, it is God's *Purposed Will* that those who love Him be justified:

*And we know that all things work together for good to those who love God, to those who are the called according to His purpose. For whom He foreknew, He also predestined to be conformed to the image of His Son, that He might be the firstborn among many brethren. Moreover who He predes-tined, these He also called; whom he called, these He also justified; and whom he justified, these he also glorified (**Ro-mans 8:28-30**).*

There is nothing anyone can do to change that. God will make it happen. Those who love God will be conformed to the image of Jesus.

We may wonder, "Why pray for what God is going to do anyway?" We ask this because once again we view prayer as a means by which we bend God to our will. As we have already learned, prayer is the means by which God bends us to His will. We pray that God accomplish what He has purposed to do in order to align our desires with His. We are to want what God wants and pray for it.

Preceptive Will

Much of what the Bible describes as God's will is not purposed. God has some desires He does not make happen.

I call this His *Preceptive Will*. He has revealed His desires through His precepts, but left us to decide whether or not we will follow them.

Matthew 7:21 speaks of the Father's *Preceptive Will*: "Not everyone who says to Me, 'Lord, Lord,' shall enter the kingdom of heaven, but he who does the will of My Father in heaven." Regrettably, many choose not to follow God's precepts. Thus they were accused of lawlessness. God wanted, or willed, that they act one way. Instead they acted another, ignoring His precepts.

God wants everyone to repent and be saved. **II Peter 3:9** says, "The Lord is not slack concerning His promise as some count slackness, but is longsuffering toward us, not willing that any should perish but that all should come to repentance." **I Timothy 2:4** adds, "God our Savior, who desires all men to be saved and to come to the knowledge of the truth." Yet, not everyone repents and, therefore, not everyone is saved.

Matthew 23:37 explains why: "O Jerusalem, Jerusalem, the one who kills the prophets and stones those who are sent to her! How often I wanted to gather your children together, as a hen gathers her chicks under her wings, but you were not willing!" God has never forced men to do what He wants. He wanted to save Jerusalem, but Jerusalem was unwilling.

Praying for God's *Preceptive Will* is what Jesus modeled in **Matthew 6:10**, "Your will be done on earth as it is in heaven." What God wants is what we should want and we should pray that it happens. Praying that God's *Preceptive Will* be accomplished helps us focus our behavior on God's desire for our lives.

Under this heading, we recognize there are some gifts God has said He wants to bestow. However, we must ask. For example, God wants us to be wise. "If any of you lacks wisdom, let him ask of God, who gives to all liberally and without reproach, and it will be given to him" (**James 1:5**). To receive God's promised wisdom, we must ask. Further, we must ask without doubting. That is, we must believe not only that He can do what we have asked, but that He will do it.

These prayers focus us on God's desires, helping us want His wants. They remind us how we are to live, helping us want to live His way. How useless our prayers would be if we prayed God's will be done while we ignored God's will for our lives?

Finally, we must never pray for something we know God does not want or will not do. After all, how could we pray that prayer in faith? Further, that denies our submission to His will.

Permissive Will

Perhaps we have the most trouble with this category of God's will. It is not about God's plans, precepts or promises. It is simply what He permits. Note **Acts 14:16**: "Who in bygone generations allowed all nations to walk in their own ways." Did God want the Gentile nations to walk in their own ways? Of course not. However, He allowed them.

On the other hand, He was not willing for Paul and his companions to travel in Bithynia: "After they had come to Mysia, they tried to go into Bithynia, but the Spirit did not permit them" (**Acts 16:7**).

No doubt, what God will permit is sometimes bound up in His *Purposed* or *Preceptive Wills*. At other times, however, it is simply allowed because God lets the world run its course.

In **Ecclesiastes 9:11**, the Preacher explained the race does not always go to the swift or the battle to the strong. Why? Time and chance are a part of our world. We must come to grips with the fact that not everything happens because God planned it to. He allows time and chance. However, only what God allows to happen occurs.

James 4:13-15 talks about this category of God's will. We must acknowledge God's control.

> *Come now, you who say, "Today or tomorrow we will go to such and such a city, spend a year there, buy and sell, and make a profit"; whereas you do not know what will happen tomorrow. For what is your life? It is even a vapor that appears for a little time and then vanishes away. Instead you ought to say, "If the Lord wills, we shall live and do this or that."*

He does not make everything happen, but what He does not allow will not happen. By praying that God's will be done, we are acknowledging His control.

Therefore, we pray regarding this will in order to seek permission. Many of our requests are made in this vein. We want something that we believe is in line with God's plans and precepts, however, we acknowledge that we do not fully know what God desires or will allow. Therefore, we petition Him. Perhaps He will allow our request. He certainly will not if we do not ask. **James 4:2** says, "Yet you do not receive, because you do not ask."

Through these prayers, we acknowledge our reliance upon God and our need for His power to allow us what we ask or desire. To pray properly for God's will we must be completely submissive to it. As much as we may want something and importune God for it, there is always something we must desire more than our request. We must want above all our desires for God to be glorified and His will done. Thus we pray, as Jesus did in the Garden, "Your will be done."

It all comes back to honoring God. No matter which concept of God's will we are addressing in prayer, it is constantly about glorifying Him, His plan, His precepts and His power.

Prayer Challenge:

What aspects of God's will should you pray for? What are some issues, whether in God's *Purposed* or *Preceptive Wills*, that you should make a regular part of your prayers to help align you with God's will?

This issue is a problem for us at times because we tend to get bogged down in thinking about how God is impacted by our prayers. Instead, how are we impacted when we pray for God's will?

Plug In:

Father in Heaven,

Holy and reverend is Your name. You are the power from which all things have their existence and continued being.

You are the Sovereign Ruler of the universe and I can do nothing without Your strength and permission.

Father, please bless me to grow in Your wisdom and knowledge. Help me pass that wisdom to others through spreading Your word.

I pray that Your word will not return to You void, but will accomplish Your plans. Use me as Your tool in those plans.

Forgive me where I have tried to be in control and taken my own path. Please, strengthen me to follow Your will.

In all things, help me submit to You.

I love You.

Through Jesus I pray,

Amen

Plugged In: High Voltage Prayer

Chapter 28

When God Says No

When God Says Yes

Have you ever noticed people never complain about a soft drink machine that spits out a drink and then gives their money back? The machine that does that is just as broken as the one that takes their money but won't give them a drink. However, they only complain that it is broken if it doesn't give the drink.

In the same manner, nobody has issues about when God says, "Yes." We act like that is the way things should be and move on.

We need to remember that God is God and we are not. We do not deserve to approach God in prayer, let alone get what we ask for. Really, it is not remarkable that God says, "No," to some of our prayers. What is remarkable is that God says, "Yes," to any of our prayers.

Therefore, when God grants our requests, we should be humbled and grateful beyond words. Yet, we should say the words. We should give thanks.

It May Not Be No

Sometimes we may think God is saying, "No," to our requests when, in fact, He is doing something completely different.

Often we have a picture in our mind of what it will look like when God says, "Yes." God, however, may grant our request without following our methods.

We find a great example of this in **Exodus 14:11**. The Israelites had groaned and cried out to God for help in the midst of their Egyptian oppression. We do not know exactly what they had in mind. However, it probably looked something like a great warrior conquering Egypt with his army and releasing the Hebrews. Whatever they envisioned, ten plagues and a trip through the Red Sea was not what they had in mind. God answers our prayers in the way that most glorifies Him. God was granting Israel their freedom, but He was doing it the way that would cause them to realize who He was. He was doing it in a way that they could never doubt how they were delivered. He was saying, "Yes." However, while they were caught between Pharaoh and the Red Sea, they thought He had said, "No."

At other times, God is not saying, "No." Instead, He is saying, "Wait."

That is the exact picture presented in **Revelation 6:10-11**:

And they cried with a loud voice, saying, "How long, O Lord, holy and true, until you judge and avenge our blood on

*those who dwell on the earth?" Then a white robe was given
to each of them; and it was said to them that they should rest
a little while longer until both the number of their fellow servants and their brethren, who would be killed as they were,
was completed.*

The martyred saints wanted God's judgment and vengeance, but God said they had to wait. It would come in His time.

We simply have to trust God that He will give us good gifts
in His good time.

Why Not

While we rarely ask, "Why?" when God grants our requests, we are full of "Why nots?" if He denies them. Perhaps
that is why the scripture provides reasons for which God says,
"No."

First and foremost, we need to remember God says, "No,"
because as God, He has the right to. I think we make a mistake
when we offer up simple platitudes to get others to carry on
when prayers do not get granted. I believe there is a very real
sense in which God says, "No," in order to teach us submission.

God is not like the mid-life crisis dad who says, "No," just
to prove he is still boss. He is a God who deserves and demands submission. Frankly, it is only submission when we are
submitting to God when He is not doing things our way.

Consider what the Hebrew writer says about Jesus in **Hebrews 5:8**. After speaking of His prayer offered with vehement
cries and tears, the scripture says, "Though He was a Son, yet
He learned obedience by the things which He suffered." That
is, Jesus prayer had been heard, but Jesus still suffered the cup
He had prayed to be removed.

Once again, we must learn that prayer is not the means by which we bend God to our will. It is the means by which we are bent to His. Perhaps one of the hardest prayer lessons to learn is that God will deny our requests to teach us obedience and submission. Keep in mind, however, that Jesus, having learned obedience through His suffering, was perfected and became the author and finisher of our salvation. That is, by learning the lessons of submission to denied requests, Jesus was exalted. We will also be exalted when we learn to humble ourselves before God, especially when He says, "No."

The entire book of Job demonstrates this. How many times did Job ask God to explain why everything was happening? Finally, God responded to Job in **Job 38-41**. However, He did not explain anything. He basically said, "I am God and you are not. Get over it and submit to Me." Job repented saying, "Therefore I abhor myself, and repent in dust and ashes" (**Job 42:6**). When Job learned this submission, God blessed him greatly. **Job 42:12** says, "Now the Lord blessed the latter days of Job more than his beginning."

Under this heading of teaching us submission, there are times when God says, "No," for very specific reasons.

James 1:6-7 says, "But let him ask in faith, with no doubting...Let not that man suppose that he will receive anything from the Lord." Sometimes God says, "No," because we did not ask in faith. As we learned in chapter 12, we need to have faith that God can do what we ask, will do what He has promised and will take care of us.

Sometimes God says, "No," because we are asking with improper motives, thinking only of our personal pleasure. **James 4:3** says, "You ask and do not receive, because you ask amiss, that you may spend it on your pleasures." Our requests must be made with God's will and with service to others in mind, not with selfish ambition or personal conceit.

At times, God says, "No," because others are involved in our prayers. We are too often myopic, unable to see past our own desires. Numerous others are involved in the answers to our prayers.

No doubt, God and His plans are involved in the answers to our prayers. When Jesus prayed the cup pass from Him, He understood that God's plans must be fulfilled. Thus He prayed, "Your will be done" (**Matthew 26:42**). God may say, "No," at times because despite our best intentions, our prayer does not correspond to His will and will not fit in with His plans.

Other people are involved. Paul prayed for salvation for his Jewish brethren in **Romans 10:1**. If they refused salvation, however, God would not save them.

Further, to whom should God say, "Yes," in the following scenario? Your father, mother, brother, sister, son or daughter is in desperate need of an organ transplant, perhaps a liver, lung or heart. You pray desperately each day that an organ can be found. However, this means a donor will have to die whose family is praying just as desperately that the donor will live. Whose request should God grant? To whom should He say, "No"? You see how tricky it is for God to listen to and answer the prayers of all His children.

Sometimes God says, "No," because He decides not to break the natural order of life. I am not saying He cannot change the natural order. Nor am I saying He never does. I am just saying He chooses not to many times. How many of our prayers are about sick loved ones? We do not want them to die. What would happen, however, if God said, "Yes," to every petition to spare someone's life? No one would die. **Hebrews 9:27** explains it is appointed for us to die. God will not always change that order just because we pray for it.

Consider also **Galatians 6:7**. "Whatever a man sows, that he will also reap." This natural law governs everything in our world. Do we believe we can smoke, drink, lounge about and overeat and then ask God for good health? We can ask, but we will likely reap what we sow. Can we spend our money recklessly, manage it poorly, live idly and then pray God grant us material prosperity? We can ask, but we will likely reap what we sow.

Finally, God says, "No," sometimes because we are not asking what is best. From heaven, God can see the big picture. We, however, can barely see our own lives properly. We sometimes make requests that seem good and right, but are skewed by our finite perceptions.

Reconsider Paul's "thorn in the flesh prayer." God told Paul, "No," even though he prayed three times for his thorn in the flesh to be removed (**II Corinthians 12:7-10**). Paul wanted the thorn removed. God recognized it helped Paul maintain his humility and therefore his salvation. If God had removed the thorn, Paul's soul would have been endangered. God did not give Paul what he asked for. Instead, He gave him something better.

We must not get angry with God when He says, "No." First, we must remember that is His right and be thankful He sometimes says, "Yes." Second, we must remember that God's goal for us is obedience that we might be perfected and exalted by Him. Therefore, when He says, "No," instead of complaining, we should consider why He denied our request and in what way we can learn submission and obedience from His denial. Through this, we too will learn obedience and through obedience, we too will be exalted by God.

Prayer Challenge:

Are there any prayers for which God has said, "No" to you? List some below. How should you respond?

Based on what you have learned in this chapter, why do you think God said, "No"? In what way do these denials teach you submission?

Plug In:

Dear God and Father of mankind,

Your power, majesty and glory are beyond my comprehension. The universe sings forth Your praises night after night.

Thank You for hearing my pleas and requests. Thank You for granting so many of them. I do not deserve Your mercy and I will praise Your lovingkindness.

Strengthen me to trust You. I pray that You help me learn from the discipline You offer through denied requests.

Father, forgive me for my lack of faith. I do believe, help my unbelief. Forgive me for my lack of trust that you will cause all

233

things to work together for good if I love You, even when You are not working things out the way I thought they should go.

Help me glorify You in all things. Thank You Father.

I love You.

In Jesus' name,

Amen

Chapter 29

Submitting To God's Will

"Help, I Will Do Anything!"

How many people have prayed this prayer? How many Christians, who ought to know better, pray this prayer?

"God, if You will just get me out of this, I will never do such and such again."

Or, "Father, if You will just give me such and such, I will do anything You ask."

What kind of God do we think we are dealing with? Does Jehovah so crave our obedience He bargains with our desires? God is God and we must obey Him no matter what is going on in our lives. We must obey Him whether He grants our requests or not.

Look again at Jesus in the Garden of Gethsemane (**Matthew 26:36-56**) and at Paul with his thorn in the flesh (**II Corinthians 12:7-10**). Jesus desired greatly for the cup to pass from Him. However, He did not bargain with the Father. "Father, keep it from hurting and I will go to the cross." He made His request, but obeyed God no matter what His answer was. Paul wanted to be rid of the thorn in the flesh. However, he did not barter, "God, take this thorn in the flesh away and I will teach every one I ever meet." He just obeyed God no matter what the answer was.

Far too many have reduced prayer to some kind of magic chant. We prayed, therefore, what we asked ought to happen. If it doesn't happen, then God must not exist. Or God must not love us. Or He must not be very powerful. At the very least, if He won't do what we want, He can't expect us to do what He wants.

It rarely occurs to us that He is God and must be allowed to act as He sees fit. He is allowed to grant our requests when He desires and deny them when He desires. He will bestow mercy and compassion on whom He desires for whatever reason He desires (**Romans 9:15**).

If He chooses not to bestow some grace upon us or if He chooses to remove some benefit, that is His option. He is God and we are not. In the beginning of the story, Job understood this. After losing everything, he said, "Naked I came from my mother's womb, and naked shall I return there. The Lord gave, and the Lord has taken away; blessed be the name of the Lord" (**Job 1:21**).

Then after he was personally attacked, he said to his wife, who encouraged him to curse God and die, "Shall we indeed accept good from God, and shall we not accept adversity" (**Job 2:10**)?

He struggled throughout the book after his three friends came and repeatedly blasted him. He thought God owed him an answer. However, as we have already seen, God simply came to him and said to buck up. God is God and Job is not God. He must simply submit to the Lord. If you don't believe me, read God's speeches in **Job 38-41**. And submit he did, no matter what. Job uttered one of the greatest verses in all the Bible. "Though He slay me, yet will I trust Him" (**Job 13:15**). Job wasn't going to bargain with God. No matter what God did, Job planned to trust and obey Him.

Prayer is not a bargaining chip. Even when making requests, it is an exercise in submission. No matter what God does with our prayers, we must continue in submission.

Heman the Ezrahite

Have you heard of this man? Probably not. Yet he sets one of the greatest examples of submission in prayer found in the Bible.

Heman wrote **Psalm 88**, which is to me, one of the most amazing psalms. Many of the psalms talk about life being bad but end with God delivering the psalmist. Note **Psalm 88**. Heman's psalm begins bad, stays bad, and ends bad.

Throughout the psalm he says:

My soul is full of troubles, and my life draws near to the grave...You have laid me in the lowest pit...Your wrath lies heavy upon me...I have called daily upon You; I have stretched out my hands to You...to You I have cried out, O Lord...Lord, why do You cast off my soul? Why do you hide Your face from me?...I suffer Your terrors...Your terrors have cut me off...

However, in the midst of all this, three keys of Heman's submission can be seen. Frankly, I am amazed by his example.

First, Heman submitted because he understood from whom salvation came. He began the psalm saying, "O Lord, God of my salvation" (vs. 1). Heman understood that no matter how bad things become, God is still God. If there is any salvation, it will come from Him. Why would he ever turn his back against God? God was his only hope. Therefore, he continued to submit. As bad as his life had become, as abandoned as he felt, he was not willing to lose eternal life to "get back at God."

Second, because Heman knew from where his salvation came, he kept a proper perspective on life. In vss. 10-12 he wrote:

> Will You work wonders for the dead? Shall the dead arise and praise You? Shall Your lovingkindness be declared in the grave? Or Your faithfulness in the place of destruction? Shall Your wonders be known in the dark? And Your righteousness in the land of forgetfulness?

Though Heman's life was bad, his concern was not about his personal welfare. His concern was how God would best be praised. If he died, as he feared he would, then he would be unable to praise God before those for whom it might make a difference. Even when Heman was certain that God had "cast off my soul," his goal was to glorify God. Amazing.

Third, because his desire was to glorify God, Heman continued to worship and serve God. Witness the psalm itself, a prayer written to petition the God of his salvation. In vs. 9, Heman says, "Lord, I have called daily upon You: I have stretched out my hands to You." In vs. 13, "But to you I have cried out, O Lord, and in the morning my prayer comes before You."

Heman was a worshipper. Even when he believed God had rejected his prayers and abandoned him, Heman continued to pray. He was going to worship and serve God daily. That is submission.

This is the kind of submission we need to have. We must never view submission as a response to granted requests and blessed lives. Rather, we must be submissive no matter what. After all, we are praying because we hope for eternal salvation, not a gilded life.

Therefore, we must ask if we have harbored any sin in our lives simply because God has not answered our prayers the way we wanted Him to. We are not hurting God by this, only ourselves. Why not confess those sins immediately and submit to God. Granted, our lives may not get any better, but our eternity certainly will.

Prayer Challenge:

Have you harbored any sin because God has not answered your prayers the way you wanted? If so, confess that to God right now and submit yourself to Him again.

Do denied requests change the evidence that has caused you to believe God exists? Do they change any of the Bible's promises?

If not, why do we often let denied request turn us from God? How can we overcome this temptation?

Plug In:

Heavenly Father,

Forgive me for my willfulness. If I have ever tried to bargain and barter my submission and obedience, wipe my slate clean. Purify my heart and make it whiter than snow.

You are the God of my salvation, my rock and my refuge in a time of trouble. Father, hear my plea.

Strengthen me to be content in whatever situation I find myself, remembering that You are with me and will not forsake me.

Help me serve You no matter what is happening in my life.

Please grant my petitions, but above all, let Your will be done and not mine. Help me boast in You and in Your grace.

I will ever declare Your praises in the congregation and in the face of Your enemies.

I love You.

By Jesus' authority I pray,

Amen

Chapter 30

Growing In Prayer

Praying Warriors

If you have read this book one day at a time, you have spent six weeks devoted to prayer. Can you see the difference in your prayer life? Have you grown? My hope and my prayer is that you can and you have.

However, if you are like me and like numerous Christians I know, you may still feel far short of a praying warrior.

Do not get bogged down. The end of this book is not the end of your growth. Really, this is only just the beginning. We have only scratched the surface of prayer. It is now up to you to continue to grow in prayer.

Like physical exercise, you must commit yourself to continue your daily PT: Prayer Training. Never forget **II Peter 1:5-8**:

> *But also for this very reason, giving all diligence, add to your faith virtue, to virtue knowledge, to knowledge self-control, to self-control perseverance, to perseverance godliness, to godliness brotherly kindness, and to brotherly kindness love. For if these things are yours and abound, you will be neither barren nor unfruitful in the knowledge of our Lord Jesus Christ.*

Christianity is about continual growth. So is prayer. You and I are not the pure paragons of prayer we would like to be, but God does not expect that of us. All He expects is growth.

I trust we are better prayers now than when we began this book. I pray that we will be better still by this time next year.

Don't Forget Your Bible

As with any aspect of Christian growth, we must not forget our Bibles. This book is not the manual for godly prayer. Hopefully, you have read it simply as a signpost pointing to the true prayer manual—God's Word.

You may desire to read through this book again or you may be done with it forever. You must, however, never abandon your Bible.

If you have not done so already, make a commitment to read from God's word daily. As you do so, pay special attention to the passages that deal with prayer.

Examine the great saints who prayed in the Bible. How did they pray? What did they say? How did their prayers impact their lives and the lives of others around them?

Pay attention to how God responded to the prayers of these great saints. When did He say, "Yes"? When did He say, "No"? Why did He give those responses?

Read the **Psalms** repeatedly. If you desire to enhance and broaden your prayer and praise language, the **Psalms** are indispensable. Further, these prayer songs provide great insight into proper attitudes, proper prayer, how God responds and how we should respond to God.

Of course, you must not forget your Bible because God's hearing you depends on your hearing Him. As we learned in an earlier chapter, we cannot expect God to listen to us if we refuse to listen to Him.

Just Pray

If we are going to grow in prayer, we must exercise in prayer. The reading of books is endless. We can take how-to courses and go to motivational meetings, but unless we pray, we will not grow in prayer.

Do not worry that you may get it wrong at times. Remember, the Holy Spirit is interceding on your behalf where you do not know what to pray (**Romans 8:26-27**). At the same time, never be complacent in your prayer growth. You must learn from your study, from your experience, and from your mistakes.

Now that you have completed this study, renew your commitment to prayer.

Pray personally. Go into your "prayer room" (**Matthew 6:6**) and pray. Praise God. Offer the thanks due Him. Make your petitions and intercessions known. Humbly confess your sins and He will forgive you. You must pray. You will never learn to pray, except by praying.

Pray with your family. Do you have a family prayer time? What a great way to teach your children to pray. At the same time, what a great way to grow in prayer. As you open your heart to God, you are opening your heart before your family, your greatest support system.

If it feels uncomfortable at first, do not worry. I remember when my wife and I first prayed together. We were extremely self-conscious. We were afraid we weren't doing it right. We certainly did not want to do any confessing in front of each other. At times I was leery of praying for her in her presence because it seemed self-serving. If I was this self-conscious, I can only imagine how my wife felt. Put yourself in her shoes. She is married to a preacher whom she is sure is analyzing everything she says to see if it is spiritual enough. Even to this day, we struggle with this. We must keep plugging away in prayer.

Pray with Christians. Find some Christian friends with which you will simply get together on a regular basis and pray. Perhaps you can circle up regularly and all of you pray. Perhaps you will get together and trade off who will pray each time. Whatever you choose, just make sure you pray with your brethren.

Further, whenever you have Christians into your home, make sure to pray with them. Do more than just a pre-meal blessing. Pray with them. If one of your brethren expresses troubles in their life, do not just promise prayers when you get home. Kneel with them in prayer right then.

Finally, pray with the congregation. Whether you are leading or being led, the prayers in the congregational assembly are not to be boring space fillers. They are not items to check off while our minds actually wander from breakfast to lunch to football to PTA. Pray, really pray. Focus on the words of the leader, pray them with him. Or word your own prayer that corresponds with what the leader is saying. Whatever you do, don't let your mind wander to and fro, pray.

In the end, remember **I Thessalonians 5:16-18**. "Rejoice always, pray without ceasing, in everything give thanks; for this is the will of God in Christ Jesus for you."

May God richly bless you, your family and your congregation as you grow in prayer. Most of all, may you richly bless God as you grow in prayer.

Prayer Challenge:

When you began this book, you made a personal commitment to work through it on a daily basis. Renew your commitment to daily Bible study and prayer.

When will you pray?

When will you study?

What will you study?

Who will you get to help hold you accountable?

What are they allowed to do to hold you accountable?

How have you grown in prayer over the past six weeks? In what areas do you still need to grow?

Plug In:

Holy and awesome God,

Teach me to pray. Help me grow in prayer. Forgive my weaknesses and help me overcome by the strength You supply.

Thank You for Your Son, whose sacrifice grants me access to Your throne of mercy and grace. Thank You for Your Spirit, who intercedes on my behalf to pray for me where I cannot. Thank You for accepting and listening to my prayers when I am so unworthy.

Help me grow in prayer and help me strengthen others in prayer.

Be with my family and with my brethren, that we may all grow together, praying more and praying with more strength. Father, help us overcome in this spiritual battle.

Above all, may You be glorified by my prayer and my life.

I love You.

In Jesus' name,

Amen

Group Discussion:

What were the most important lessons you learned about prayer this week?

How did this week's readings help your prayer life?

What advice would you give others based on this week's reading to help them pray?

With what issues do you need help or prayers based on this week's reading?

How can we use singing as part of our prayer lives?

What does it mean to pray for God's will and why should we?

How must we respond when God denies our requests? What advice do you have to help people respond properly?

Why is bargaining with God an improper approach to prayer?

What advice do you have for others to help with continued prayer growth?

YOUR FIRST 10 DAYS AS A CHRISTIAN

Tired of losing new converts out the back door? _Your First 10 Days as a Christian_ is a powerful tool for every personal worker and every congregation. Start your new converts off on the right foot the very first day. This dvd is power-packed with 10 lessons, each less than 15 minutes, to help the new convert get on God's path and stay there. Don't face another baptism without this new dvd on hand.

"If you do personal evangelism or teach home Bible studies, you would do well to follow up the conversions with Edwin Crozier's new DVD, **Your First 10 Days as a Christian**. It's fundamental and biblical. It's simple, but powerful. We've already ordered it where I am."

Dee Bowman, Pasadena, TX

"Satan is after new converts. **Your First 10 Days as a Christian** is a powerful defensive weapon in protecting new Christians from his assaults and a great way to get them off to a fast start. We give a copy to every person we baptize whether young or old because Crozier's DVD fills a critical gap in their lives."

Max Dawson, Beaumont, TX

"I just watched the **Your First 10 Days** videos. They are right on target with what needs to be said to new babes in Christ. Years ago I wrote a series of lessons called 'The New Me' that I try to teach to new Christians. But this will now be my First Step in the process of taking them from milk to meat."

Rick Lanning, New Hope, MN

Order at www.streamsidesupplies.com

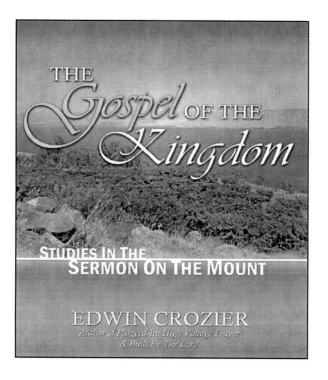

THE GOSPEL OF THE KINGDOM

Who has not spent time within the Sermon on the Mount? Who has not been refreshed, challenged, and rebuked by Jesus in this sermon? Yet we keep coming back to it. We are drawn to it, knowing it contains the concentrated essence of what Jesus wants us to be. For whatever reason we come to the sermon, if we study it deeply, we cannot leave unchanged. No wonder Matthew called it "the gospel of the kingdom." Take a fresh look at the greatest sermon ever preached in Edwin Crozier's book, complete with guides for personal daily devotion and weekly group discussion.

Order anywhere books are sold or directly from the publisher at
www.streamsidesupplies.com

GIVE ATTENTION TO READING

Sometimes we all need a little help in our daily Bible study. *Give Attention to Reading* is that help. Dividing the New Testament into weekday readings for six-months, this book provides the Bible student with guidance and direction to develop a daily discipline of study.

Each weekday reading covers two chapters of the New Testament. Complete with a place for notes, study questions and even a weekly group discussion guide, this tool is a must for anyone trying to develop or improve their Bible reading and study habit.

Begin in Luke and then work your way through the entire New Testament as you follow this guide to help you develop your daily discipline.

Order anywhere books are sold or directly from the publisher at
www.streamsidesupplies.com

WALKS WITH GOD

Every day thousands of Christians hit the gym, go for a run, take a swim or practice Pilates. We want to take care of our bodies so they will be around for a while. Regrettably, too many are missing out on the greatest exercise—walking with God. It's good for the heart, good for the soul and, yes, even good for the body. It is the only exercise with everlasting benefits.

Edwin Crozier's *Walks with God* provides you with a month of godly exercise, stretching your spiritual muscles and challenging you to move your relationship with God to the next level. Whether you are already walking with God, just getting started on your exercise regimen or struggling to maintain your workout discipline, *Walks with God* will help you get on the right track and stay there.

Order anywhere books are sold or directly from the publisher at
www.streamsidesupplies.com

LaVergne, TN USA
18 August 2009
155106LV00001B/36/A